100 WA
Yorkshi

The Crowood Press

First published in 1991 by
The Crowood Press Ltd
Ramsbury, Marlborough
Wiltshire SN8 2HR

This impression 1994

British Library Cataloguing-in-Publication Data
100 walks in Yorkshire (Vol I).
1. Yorkshire – Visitor's guides
914.283904859

ISBN 1 85223 417 2

All maps by Sharon Perks

Cover picture by John Cleare

Typeset by Carreg Ltd, Nailsea, Bristol

Printed and bound in Great Britain by
Biddles Ltd, Guildford and King's Lynn

THE CONTRIBUTORS

Glen Hood

John Severs

Paul Sherwood

Charles Emett

John Bennington

Margaret Ryder

Paul Beales

Lee Davison

CONTENTS

North-East

North-West

32. ... and longer version 8m (13km)
33. Whixley and Allerton 5m (8km)
34. Hovingham 5m (8km)
35. Terrington 5m (8km)
36. Slingsby 5m (8km)
37. Thirsk 5m (8km)
38. Barton $5^1/_2$m (9km)
39. Bilsdale West Moor 6m (10km)
40. Sutton Bank $6^1/_2$m (10km)
41. Osmotherley $6^1/_2$m (10km)
42. Ingleby Greenhow 7m (11km)
43. Great Ayton 7m (11km)
44. Osmotherley/Beacon Hill 7m (11km)
45. Hawnby 7m (11km)
46. Sheriff Hutton 7m (11km)
47. Sutton Bank 7m (11km)
48. Ampleforth 7m (11km)
49. Welburn 7m (11km)
50. Kepwick 7m (11km)
51. Kirkham Priory 8m (13km)
52. Kilburn 8m (13km)
53. Castle Howard 8m (13km)
54. Nunnington 8m (13km)
55. Rievaulx 8m (13km)
56. Clay Bank 8m (13km)
57. Bilsdale 9m (14.5km)
58. Hovingham 10m (16km)
59. Stokesley 10m (16km)
60. Clay Bank Area 10m (16km)
61. Battersby 14m (22.5km)

South-West

62. York Bar Walls 3m (5km)
63. Tadcaster 6m (9.5km)
64. York 7m (11km)
65. Fishlake 7m (11km)
66. Stamford Bridge 7m (11km)
67. Acaster Selby 7m (11km)

68. Nether Poppleton 8m (13km)
69. Bishop Wilton 8m (13km)
70. Long Marston 8m (13km)
71. Bubwith – Route 1 8m (13km)
72. Bubwith – Route 2 9m (14.5km)
73. Howden 10m (16km)
74. Pocklington 11m (17.5km)

South-East

75. Welton Dale 4m (6.5km)
76. Bempton 5m (8km)
77. Humber Bridge 5m (8km)
78. … and longer version 12m (19km)
79. Skidby 6m (9.5km)
80. Beverley 6m (9.5km)
81. Hornsea 6m (9.5km)
82. Welton 7m (11km)
83. Bracey Bridge 7m (11km)
84. Driffield 7m (11km)
85. Market Weighton 7m (11km)
86. Beeford 7m (11km)
87. Millington Dale $7^3/_4$m (12.5km)
88. Wharram Percy 8m (13km)
89. Spurn Head 8m (13km)
90. Bainton 8m (13km)
91. Paull 8m (13km)
92. Brough–Ferriby–Welton $8^3/_4$m (14km)
93. South Cave 9m (14.5km)
94. Withernsea 9m (14.5km)
95. Danes Dyke 9m (14.5km)
96. Swine 9m (14.5km)
97. Huggate 10m (16km)
98. North Newbald 10m (16km)
99. Lockington 11m (17.5km)
100. South Cave and Brantingham 12m (19km)

INTRODUCTION

The Crowood Press are greatly indebted to our contributors who walked cheerfully all over the county researching the walks for this book. It must be borne in mind that while all the details of these walks (hedges, fences, stiles, and so on) were correct at the time of going to print, the countryside is constantly changing and we cannot be held responsible if details in the walk descriptions are found to be inaccurate. We would be grateful if walkers would let us know of any major alterations to the walks described so that we may incorporate any changes in future editions. Please write to THE 100 WALKS SERIES, The Crowood Press Ltd, Gipsy Lane, Swindon, Wiltshire SN2 6DQ. Walkers are strongly advised to take with them the relevant map for the area and Ordnance Survey maps are recommended for each walk. The walks are organised by dividing the county arbitrarily into four areas – north-east, north-west, south-west and south-east – and are then listed by length – from approximately 3 miles to 12 miles. No attempt has been made to estimate how long the walks will take as this can vary so greatly depending on the strength and fitness of the walkers and the time spent exploring the points of interest highlighted. Nearly all the walks are circular and the majority offer a recommended place to seek refreshments. Telephone numbers of these pubs and cafés are included in case you want to check on opening times, meals available, and so on.

We hope you enjoy exploring the county of Yorkshire in the best possible way – on foot – and ask that you cherish its beautiful places by always remembering the country code:

Enjoy the country and respect its life and work
Guard against all risk of fire
Fasten all gates
Keep dogs under close control
Keep to public footpaths across all farmland
Use gates and stiles to cross field boundaries
Leave all livestock, machinery and crops alone
Take your litter home
Help to keep all water clean
Protect wildlife, plants and trees
Make no unnecessary noise

Good walking.

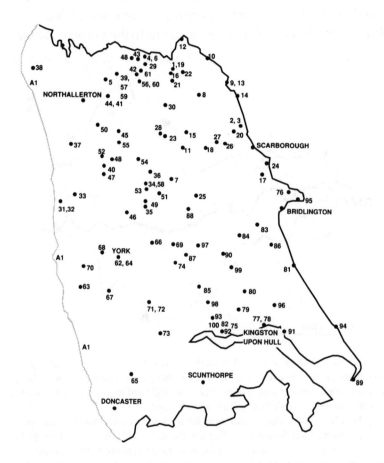

Walk 1   DANBY AND CASTLETON   4m (6.5km)

Maps: OS Sheets Landranger 94; Outdoor Leisure 26.

Moderate walk, including woodland, moorland, farm tracks and arable land. Total climbing over the whole route 180m.

Start: At 685084, in Castleton adjacent to the railway station.

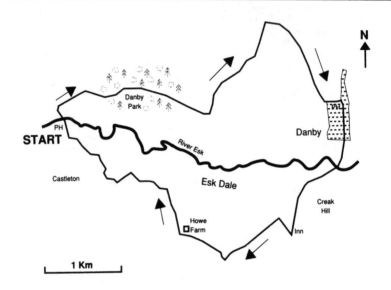

Cross the river and follow the road under the railway bridge. Immediately after passing the entrance to the old quarry buildings turn right up a grass bank, follow the flagged footpath uphill where it joins a farm track. Turn right and follow a well-defined track which continues through Danby Park, a birch wood.

After leaving the wood continue on the track across open moorland for about $\frac{1}{4}$ mile, then turn left off this track to follow a bridle path uphill. This passes the right-hand corner of the largest enclosed field and continues uphill passing the left-hand side of the smallest enclosed field. A few yards past this field the path veers left. Do not follow the path to the left. Continue straight ahead and cross the field's wire fence directly ahead. The path here is a little indistinct but aim for the top left-hand side of the field in front, which has reverted to moorland grasses. A farm gate then opens on to a green lane. Follow this to its end and turn right along a further broad green lane passing Hollin Top Farm on your right. Continue along the farm driveway to join the road, turn left and walk into the village of Danby. In front of you is the 'Duke of Wellington' public house. The road ahead leads to the North York Moors National Park Centre at **Danby Lodge** and to the fourteenth century **Duck Bridge** and **Danby Castle**, all about 1 mile away.

Turn right and downhill from the public house, with the village hall on your left. Cross the railway bridge near Danby Station and the bridge over the River Esk. This is about your half way point. Go a few hundred yards on this road to reach the hamlet of Ainthorpe. Take the left fork at the fire station and continue uphill to the '**Fox and Hounds**' public house. Cross the green directly opposite the pub and descend via a broad green track, to join the road. Cross into the field on the left over a stile. The path continues over four fields and joins a road at Danby Vicarage.

Turn left and continue along the road. Directly opposite the vicarage climb over the steps in the drystone wall into a field. To your right you will see further steps into the next field. The buildings of Howe Farm can be seen directly ahead and the path passes through the grassed yard of the farm to reach the road beyond. Turn right along the road and where it joins another road turn left across the 'Howe' following a footpath past the war memorial. The path descends and crosses the Danby Beck over a footbridge and reaches Castleton opposite the Church. Follow the road uphill into the centre of the village and turn right at the tearooms. The road descends into the valley passing the cricket field and back to your starting point.

POINTS OF INTEREST:
Danby Lodge – A 17th century shooting lodge, adapted as a visitor centre for the National Park. Car parking. Half a mile east of Danby.
Duck Bridge – Typical 'pack-horse bridge' built in 1386.
Danby Castle – A 14th century castle, once the home of Katherine Parr, the last wife of Henry VIII. Now a farm. One mile east of Danby.
Fox and Hounds – The oldest part of the pub dates from 1555, Oliver Cromwell is reputed to have called here during the Civil War.

REFRESHMENTS:
The Fox and Hounds, Ainthorpe (tel no: 0287 60218).
The Duke of Wellington, Danby (tel no: 0287 60351).
Danby Lodge Moors Centre (tel no: 0287 60540).

Walks 2 and 3   **CLOUGHTON**   4m (6.5km) or 7m (11km)
Maps: OS Sheets Landranger 101; Outdoor Leisure 27.
*A short but beautiful walk, easily extended, mainly along cliff top
and disused railway. Good underfoot. One moderate hill.*
Start: The end of Newlands Avenue, Cloughton, overlooking the
cliffs at Cloughton Wyke.

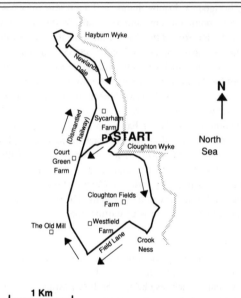

Walk back along the quiet and narrow road towards Cloughton. Cross the railway
bridge and immediately turn right through a small gate. Descend to the **disused railway**
by path or steps and walk northwards. A bridge takes the railway across the road to
Sycarham Farm to pass through a narrow valley. The pretty North End House is passed
and **Hayburn Wyke Hotel** is reached. Pass through the gate across the railway and turn
right along the road which bends left to the hotel. Walk ahead past the left-hand side
of the hotel and cross the stile by a gate. A grass track bears right, and a little downhill,
to reach another stile and gate and enters woodland.

    Cross the stile and pause at the National Trust notice board which gives details of
Hayburn Wyke. A path goes left from the track, downhill, to reach a wider track.

Continue ahead with Hayburn Beck on your left. A closer view of the beck can be seen by walking a short distance along a narrow path and later returning to the track. The beck descends through the beautiful woodland, with a series of small waterfalls. The beach is reached after crossing a footbridge over the beck.

Return across the bridge. You are now on the **Cleveland Way**, and a signposted path goes left, uphill, off the track. Steps help. A short diversion can be made along a path passed part way up to view a small pond. Return to the Way. Before reaching a gate, turn left up more steps to follow the clifftop path. For a time, bushes hide the view, but soon it becomes excellent as we reach our highest point. Steps help us down and up a steep sided little valley and across a small stream, before we reach the final descent to Cloughton Wyke. Access to the rocky beach here is easy and the car is close by.

To extend the walk, start by walking along the clifftop southward to reach a narrow road which leads to Burniston and, just before the village, gain access to the railway by the side of the bridge. Continue along this to Hayburn Wyke.

POINTS OF INTEREST:

The Hayburn Wyke Hotel – Reputed to be a smugglers' haunt, it once provided accommodation for passengers arriving by rail. A network of paths was established to help them enjoy the valley.

Hayburn Wyke – A beautiful woodland area owned by the National Trust. The beck tumbles down the centre of it to reach the sea.

The disused railway line and **the Cleveland Way** – Help to provide a series of excellent circular walks between Scarborough and Whitby. One local group hopes to restore the railway. Much effort is being made to improve the Cleveland Way.

REFRESHMENTS:

The Hayburn Wyke Hotel (tel no: 0723 870202) bar meals and restaurant.
There are several inns and shops in Cloughton.

Walk 4   **MAY BECK**   5m (8km)

Maps: OS Sheets Landranger 94; Outdoor Leisure 27.

An easy walk, a little gradual climbing, forest, streams, waterfalls.

Start: At 893025, the May Beck car park.

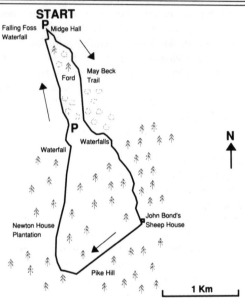

The North York Moors National Park publish a **May Beck Trail** guide and some of this walk is along the Trail. Do not be confused by trying to follow the Trail waymarking!

Walk back out of the car park. As soon as you cross the bridge take the footpath upwards to your right and continue along this for a few hundred yards keeping the beck on your right. Go through a gate and you will see a No 14 Trail marker post. You soon reach a stone footbridge marked 'Hunters Steen'. The easy to follow path continues for about $^1/_2$ mile, crossing many stone and timber bridges until you come to the open moor at **John Bond's Sheep House**. The Trail goes straight on here but you need to follow the footpath signed to the right, up into the forest towards Pike Hill.

This is a gradual climb for $^1/_2$ mile following a well-defined path through mature coniferous woodland to reach the disused quarries on Pike Hill. These are on the Whinstone Ridge, an outcrop of igneous rock which runs for 300 miles from Mull, outcropping at several places on the North York Moors where it was quarried for road materials due to its hardness.

Turn right at the quarries and follow the forest road for 300yds, turning right again and back into the forest at a signpost. After a matter of yards you are redirected left. Continue downhill for a little over $\frac{1}{2}$ mile, leaving the forest at a gate. A few yards further on, on your left you will see an interesting little waterfall, before you cross the beck. Go uphill to join the forest road.

Almost straight ahead a signed footpath leads you above Old May Beck Farm and downwards to Midge Hall, a disused house above Falling Foss waterfall.

The return to May Beck car park is made by following the 'Coast to Coast Walk' signed footpath from the bridge at Midge Hall. This takes you upstream, crossing a ford and following the beckside path through old woodland full of grey squirrels.

POINTS OF INTEREST:
May Beck Trail Leaflet – Published by and available from the North York Moors National Park Information Service.
Helmsley (tel no: 0439 70657).
Danby Moors Centre (tel no: 0287 60654).
Sutton Bank Information Centre (tel no: 0845 597426).
John Bond's Sheep House – One point on the first of our circles. This circle makes up a Forestry Commission Nature Trail. Above the stream you pass a mini coal mine and on the moorland track a small rock on your left is Wade's Wife's head! Wade was a legendary giant.

REFRESHMENTS:
The nearest shops, inns etc are in Ruswarp or Sleights, both about 3 miles away.

Maps: OS Sheets Landranger 94; Outdoor Leisure 27.

An easy walk – arable, moorland and marginal forestry – passing several geological sites.

Start: At 853938, the Hole of Horcum car park.

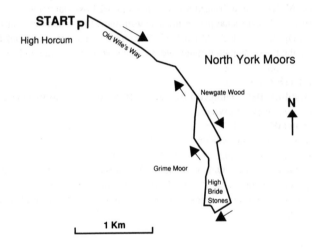

About half way between Whitby and Pickering, two miles south of the Fylingdales Early Warning Station is the spectacular geological feature, The Hole of Horcum, a three hundred feet deep, steep-sided basin, a popular site for Hang Glider enthusiasts.

On the opposite side of the road to the depression a hundred yards north of the car park there is a public footpath sign leading you along a tarmac covered farm track. Do not be deterred by the 'Private Road' sign a few yards further on. Follow this track for a little less than a mile to a point where the farm track starts to go down a steep hill. To your left you will see a small glacial valley with a reservoir at its end. Ahead of you, you will see another geological feature, 'Blakey Topping', and beyond that five or six square miles of Langdale Forest. When the farm track descends, continue through a gate ahead and contour around the top of Newgate Brow. After $^1/_4$ mile you will see footpath signs (yellow arrows), one pointing to your right across a field, the other pointing downhill to Newgate Foot Farm. In the corner of a small field just before Blakey Topping you can see three Early Bronze Age standing stones, all that remains of a 50ft diameter stone circle.

Continue contouring the ridge until you reach a gate at the edge of the wood. A bureaucratic dog-leg on this public right of way causes a little confusion: follow the woodland track for 200yds to a point where you will see further yellow arrows – follow the one to the right. This takes you a few yards through trees, and over a stile to join the forest perimeter track at the other side of the ancient earthwork. Turn left and follow this track for $\frac{1}{2}$ mile. Just after a slight dip, you will notice a footpath leading right, taking you through heather. Follow this for $\frac{1}{4}$ mile until you see the National Trust footpaths around the 'Bridestones'. These are strangely shaped, weathered Corallian limestone rocks standing about 20ft high.

When you join the National Trust footpath turn right, dropping down towards a stream and back up again. After the third or so rock, the National Trust path turns left and continues its circuit of the whole estate. If you have the time and energy it's well worth visiting all the stones. If it is time for you to return you must take the right-hand fork on a lesser path which takes you $\frac{1}{2}$ mile to the head of Dovedale Griff. Follow this small stream until you reach a stile to the left of a small pond in the first arable field. To the right of the pond is a gate with yellow arrow footpath markings. Go through this gate and turn left, keeping the field edge on your left. You will come to a wire fence with a gate and a stile, go through or over and bear right aiming for the next stile 200yds ahead of you. This brings you back to your outward route above Newgate Foot Farm. Turn left and walk for a little over a mile back to the car park.

REFRESHMENTS:
The Saltersgate Inn, (half a mile north) (tel no: 0751 60237).
The Fox and Rabbit, (three miles south) (tel no: 0751 60213).

Walk 6　　　　　　MAY BECK　　　　　　6m (9.5km)

Maps: OS Sheets Landranger 94; Outdoor Leisure 27.

A 'figure of eight' route mainly by streams and through woodland.

Start: The car park at May Beck.

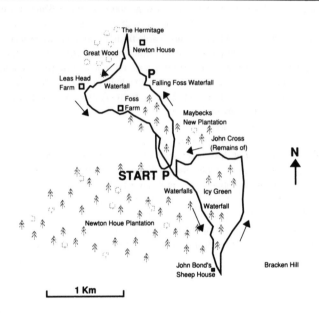

To the south-east of the car park a path leads upwards along the left-hand bank of a stream and above a waterfall. This delightful path continues to John Bond's Sheep House, (*see* Walk 4) a ruin now, where open moorland is reached. Turn left and follow the path just inside the fence by the edge of the woodland up to a stile. Cross and continue along a wider track North to a small group of trees and a gate on the left. Note the stump of John's Cross. Turn left through the gate and soon take a distinct, but narrow, footpath to the left and cross a stile. A fence is on your left for a few yards before you descend a hill, bearing left, to reach a stile and the road near the car park.

　　Perhaps after refreshment, follow the path northwards from the car park starting by the eastern side of the stream, then taking a few steps up to the right before crossing a stile. An interesting swampy area is passed on your right. At a track junction, turn left down to the stream. Cross by using the flat rocks as stepping stones. If too deep, return to the junction and turn left to the road and descend. **Falling Foss** waterfall is reached. Cross the footbridge and climb the path uphill and continue well above the eastern bank of the stream up to a large hollowed-out rock. This is the **Hermitage**.

Take the path sharp left downhill and cross a footbridge. Look for the not too clear start of a path just across a small stream here, on your right. Cross the stream and follow this very slightly difficult path as it bears left uphill through trees to a stile. Cross and walk through Leas Head farmyard. Keep to the track on your left which descends slightly downhill to a ford. A small lake is largely hidden on your right. Turn left at a track junction and walk to Foss Farm. A footpath leaves the track on your left just past the farm. You should note that you are bearing right. Turn left at a track which leads downhill back to the car park.

POINTS OF INTEREST:
Falling Foss – One of Yorkshire's higher waterfalls. Another nature trail starts here.
The Hermitage and the two seats above – Believed to have been carved by a local mason, called Jeffrey. George Chubb, a local teacher, was GC.

REFRESHMENTS:
The Flask Inn, on the Scarborough road, (tel no: 0723 880305).
Robin Hood's Bay, Ruswarp, Sleights and Whitby are not too distant.

Walk 7   **MALTON AND LOW HUTTON**   7m (11km)

Maps: OS Sheets Landranger 100; Pathfinder SE 66/76 & 67/77.

Fairly gentle walking, mostly flat, part riverside, and including a length of quiet road.

Start: Park by the Railway Station in Malton.

Walk to the left of **Malton** bus station and take the path along the River Derwent side on the right just before the bridge. Reach the road and walk over the level crossing. Continue round to the left and walk through the car park on your right. Turn left along the road to the footpath on the right by a lamp-post where the road bends. Turn right at a path junction. The path widens and there is a pleasant pond on the left. Cross the next road and take the left-hand of the twin tracks opposite to a stile on the left. Walk along the clear track to the opposite corner of the field and maintain direction to a stile just to the right of **Star Cottage Stables**.

Turn right along the track and then left along the enclosed path just before the golf course. This does tend to get overgrown. If it is too bad, divert round it. Bear right along the track over the golf course. This bears left between trees over a bridge and near to a lake. Cross the stile on the right and bear left to another. Turn left along the fence to use the pleasanter permissive path and turn right along the raised grassy area to woodland. Walk left of an old gate post and bear left on an indistinct path uphill through the wood. Beware of nettles! The path quickly opens out and, after leaving the wood, the quiet Menethorpe Lane is reached. Follow this for a little over a mile, past Menethorpe Hall and a right-hand bend. As the road bends sharply left, take the track which bears right, down to a suspension bridge over the Derwent at Low Hutton.

You may like to try this, but then walk North towards Malton on the Eastern bank of the river, underneath the railway bridge and past Cherry Islands. Keep to a path close to the riverside crossing stiles or passing through gates. At one point, the river and the railway sandwich the path which becomes narrow and goes between bushes and rails for a short distance. This gets just a little overgrown. Just before Malton is reached, there are boats on the river. They cannot travel far unless the locks are repaired. A gate opens on to a short track near the bridge at the start. Turn right to the station.

POINTS OF INTEREST:

Malton – A very busy town on the northern bank of the River Derwent close to its junction with the Rye. Little remains of its castle.

Star Cottage Stables – Reminds us that horse racing is very important locally. This is centred on Norton, Malton's twin town which is on the south bank of the river.

REFRESHMENTS:

There are plenty of inns providing refreshment, a small café in the railway station and a popular fish and chip shop on the main road in Norton.

Walk 8   **DANBY RIGG AND LITTLE FRYUPDALE**   7m (11km)
Maps: OS Sheets Landranger 94; Outdoor Leisure 26.
Moderate walk, including moorland, farm tracks and arable land. Nearly 1000ft of climbing.
Start: At 717083, the Danby Lodge Moors Centre car park.

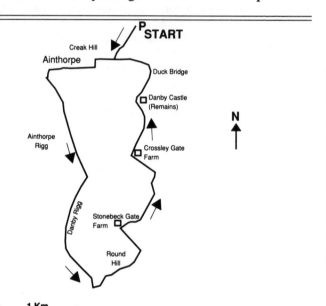

Cross the River Esk at the southern end of the Moors Centre grounds via the footbridge. Continue uphill, crossing the railway line to where the path ends at Easton Lane. Turn right and follow the lane for about 200 yards.

A short distance past Kadelands House there is a stile on the left. Cross this and follow the well-used footpath straight ahead until the corner of a field is reached. Turn right here, keeping the hedge to your left. Continue for a further 200yds to a stile over a fence.

Continue in the same direction keeping the wall on your right until a stile is reached. Cross this and a few yards further on another stile leads into a farm lane. Turn right and follow the lane until the hamlet of Ainthorpe is reached.

Turn left at the road and continue uphill past the Fox and Hounds pub until the road

26

bends sharply left. At this point follow the bridleway across Ainthorpe Rigg, shortly passing through a gate. The path eventually reaches the edge of the Rigg overlooking Little Fryupdale. Do not descend, but follow the path which contours around **Danby Rigg** and joins the Rosedale to Fryup road at the top of the bank.

Turn right and walk 100yds to a public bridleway sign indicating the path down to Fryup. Follow the path, passing through a gate in the drystone wall at the moor edge and descend into the valley. You continue through grass pasture via another gate and gate hole to join the road at Fairy Cross Plain.

Turn left and follow the road downhill to Stonebeck Gate Farm. Enter the farmyard and follow the bridleway which passes through arable land until Foresters Lodge is reached.

Immediately before the house is reached cross into the field via a gate and skirt around the right-hand side of the farm. Pass through another gate and descend into the valley to cross Little Fryup Beck. Follow the path uphill to reach the motor road at a point to the left of Crossley Gate Farm.

Turn right and follow the road passing **Danby Castle**. Turn right at the T-junction and descend into the valley via a narrow winding lane. Pass **Duck Bridge** and arrive back in Easton Lane, following the field path back to your starting point.

POINTS OF INTEREST:
Danby Rigg – Site of Bronze Age settlement covered by over 300 small cairns. At 708065, a standing stone 5ft high is the sole survivor of a 42ft diameter circle. At the centre two urn burials c1000BC were excavated.
Danby Castle – Built around 1300 to a rectangular design around a courtyard. A farmhouse now occupies the southern part of the buildings. The great hall, kitchen and other rooms are still standing. Katherine Parr lived here before becoming Henry VIII's last wife. The arms of Neville, Lord Latimer are visible from the road. Access to the castle may be gained by enquiring at the farmhouse.
Duck Bridge – Pack-horse bridge built in 1386 to gain access to the castle. Neville coat of arms on south side. It was restored in 18th century by a local mason called George Duck.

REFRESHMENTS:
The Fox and Hounds, Ainthorpe (tel no: 0287 60218).

Walk 9   ROBIN HOOD'S BAY TO RAVENSCAR   7m (11km)

Maps: OS Sheets Landranger 94; Outdoor Leisure 27.
Moderate, steep little bays, field paths can be muddy.
Start: At 950055, the car park at Robin Hood's Bay.

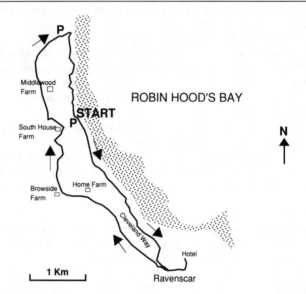

From the car park, walk down the steep street of **Robin Hood's Bay** towards the beach. The red-tiled houses seem to stand on each other's shoulders. There is no harbour and boats are launched either from the beach or, at high tide, from the main street. Opposite the Bay Hotel, climb Covet Hill Steps, signposted for the Cleveland Way. Follow the narrow path to the left behind the upper level of cottages out on to the clifftop. Continue along the clifftop path to Boggle Hole. The youth hostel was once a mill. 'Boddle' is a local name for a hobgoblin, sometimes helpful, sometimes mischievous.

Clamber out of Boggle Hole, following the Cleveland Way clifftop footpath, sheltered by blackthorn and furze bushes. At Stoupe Beck Sands, take the paved path steeply up from the beach to the bend below the second farm. Turn left at a stile with a footpath sign, and follow the path in the direction of **Ravenscar**, the hotel prominent on the headland, with a 9 hole golf course below it. Low tide exposes great shelves and slabs of pink coloured rock. The path turns up by fields to a cart track, partly paved with Ravenscar bricks. Turn left and continue to Ravenscar, emerging on the road near the Information Office.

Turn left, and go down the drive towards the Raven Hall Hotel. On the right is a Stables Bar, bar meals available, which welcomes walkers. This is the termination of the 40 mile Lyke Wake Walk. On the left of the drive, the golf course access road gives a fine view back to Robin Hood's Bay.

Return to the Information Office and turn right on the track by which you entered Ravenscar. Turn left, then right on the old railway track. Pass the overgrown ruins of the brick and alum works. The railway track has sudden ups and downs due to coastal erosion. After 2 miles, turn right at the farm and riding centre. Walk down a bridleway through meadows to a footbridge, then follow the path through trees up to the road. This part can be muddy.

Turn right. Go along the road to the parking place above Boggle Hole. Turn left between farm buildings on a cart track. Go down the Mill Beck, cross by the footbridge, then clamber up to the road. Turn right and continue to the disused railway line. Climb up and walk along the line, the village of Fylingthorpe to the left. Where the track comes to a road, turn right and go down to your starting point.

POINTS OF INTEREST:

Robin Hood's Bay – A picturesque, popular fishing village. It features as Bramblewick in Leo Walmsley's book, *Three Rivers*. The area known as The Dock still has a few fishing vessels. The cliffs are well-known to fossil hunters but, be warned, the tide rises fast.

Ravenscar – Raven Hall Hotel is built on the site of a Roman signal station. A private house was built in 1774. George III spent some time here being treated for his madness.

Walk 10   **WHITBY**   7m (11km)

Maps: OS Sheets Landranger 94; Outdoor Leisure 27.

*Fairly gentle walking, generally good underfoot, along clifftop,
disused railway, and through old streets. Good views.*

Start: The Abbey Plain car park in Whitby.

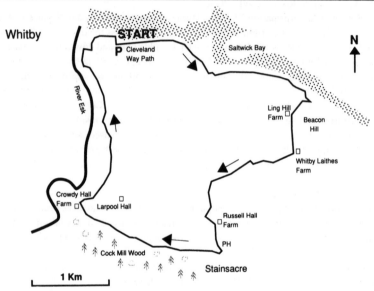

From the car park walk across the grass to the clifftop and take the enclosed Cleveland
Way path in front of the Coastguard look-out station. Boards give a good walking
surface up to Saltwick Nab holiday park. The beach here is accessible along two paths,
one of which leads to a National Trust owned area of geological interest. Follow the
path round the cliff side of the camp and cross the stile to continue along the quieter
clifftop above Saltwick Bay to the well-sheltered Fog Siren building. Use the path on
its left and cross the grass field to the stile to the right of the lighthouse wall.

Turn right along the road here and reach Ling Hill Farm. Just before the farm, pass
through the gate on the left and then go through the gate ahead. Turn right, uphill, by
the fence and go through a gate on the right near the top of the field. Continue on the
wide track over Beacon Hill to Whitby Laithes Farm. Turn right along the farm road

to Hawkser Lane. Turn right along the road and quickly left through a gate immediately before the farm. After more gates, the path goes ahead and downhill, across to a field corner and a stile and footbridge. A little way up, cross a stile on the left and head across a field towards the right of a hedge. Cross the stile on the right just before this, and try to avoid brambles for a few yards. A gap on the right gives access to the A171. Cross and turn left along the pavement. Go right along the road into Stainsacre. Just after the Windmill Inn, go under the bridge and gain access to the disused railway on your left. Turn left towards **Whitby**. The track passes through a wooded area and ends just before the viaduct over the River Esk.

Turn left on to the road, having crossed a road bridge. Go left under the bridge along Larpool Lane. Pass Larpool Hall and the cemetery, and cross the A171 bearing left down Church Street. Cross the smaller bridge over Spital Beck and walk alongside Eskside Wharf. Note a commemorative stone here. Turn left past old shops and the Captain Cook Memorial Museum, going down Grape Lane. Cross the street which leads to the bridge and walk along Sandgate. Bear right at the small Town Hall, partly used by traders, and walk left down Church Street up to the famous steps. Newcomers remember to count! Pass Caedmon Cross and turn left, in front of St Mary's Church. Go right along the cliff top. The views are superb here. Shortly, turn right to your car.

POINTS OF INTEREST:

Whitby – An extremely historic town, apart from its association with Dracula, whose trail can be followed! Many of the old shops sell craftware, including jet for which Whitby was a thriving centre. Captain Cook sailed from here. St Hilda founded the Abbey in 657AD. (Open Good Friday – 30 September 10–6pm, winter 10–1pm and 2–4pm). St Mary's church was furnished largely by shipwrights and has likenesses to the inside of a sailing ship inside. The harbour is well used.

REFRESHMENTS:

Readily available from the many cafés and inns in Whitby as well as the Windmill Inn at Stainsacre.

Walk 11   THORNTON DALE   7m (11km)

Maps: OS Sheets Landranger 100; Pathfinder SE 88/98.

An easy, fairly level walk with one climb and some unavoidable road walking.

Start: Thornton Dale car park.

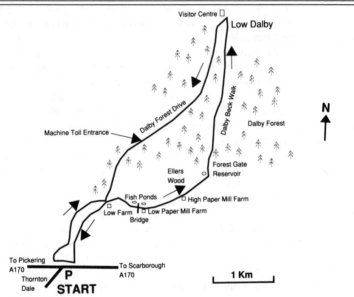

From **Thornton Dale** take the footpath to the village centre where you go right along Chestnut Avenue (A170) and turn left into Brook Lane near the grammar school. Where the lane bends left, bear right past Brook Motors and up an enclosed path signed 'Private Road – Public Footpath Only'. Turn right at the road ahead and 50 yards along it take the upper road on your left signed 'Etherburn 1 mile'. At the hamlet turn left at the Saxon church and take a gated road alongside Thornton Beck. After $^1/_4$ mile you bridge the beck and go left with the beck now on your left. Pass Low, and then **High Paper Mill Farms** and eventually enter **Dalby Forest**.

     Continue northwards for $1^1/_2$ miles along a flat, forest walk with, after $^1/_2$ mile, Dalby Beck on your left to reach Low Dalby Village, a good half way butty stop. Leave Low Dalby opposite some forest workers' houses along Dalby Forest Drive, climbing steadily, for 2 miles to a car toll. Continue along the road for a further $\frac{1}{2}$ mile and where it makes a right-angled bend right bear left into a woodland and follow the signposted footpath through the wood and into a field. Keep on the path down the field side, known locally as Kirkdale Slade back into Ellerburn hamlet. Cross the bridge opposite the church, go through a farmyard with Low Farm on your left and turn right beside a footpath sign fixed to an outbuilding. Now follow yellow arrow markers southwards over stiled fields to Victory Mill. There, go through a private car park, passing the mill on your right, to Beck Hole Cottage and turn right to cross the beck on a footbridge. Continue past thatched Beck Isle Cottage and along the beck side path to the main road. Turn right along it, retracing your steps to the car park at the end of a very pleasant walk.

POINTS OF INTEREST:

Thornton Dale – Often referred to as the prettiest village in Yorkshire.

There is a series of fish ponds on private land on the opposite bank of Thornton Beck to the route as it passes Low Paper Mill Farm.

High Paper Mill Farm – Where once paper was manufactured from rags there is now a fish farm.

Dalby Forest – Covers an area of 8650 acres. Some of the trees planted in it close to the route are named for the edification of interested walkers.

The Visitor Centre at Low Dalby, which is open to the public from April to October, has an information room and a museum. The village itself was built in 1949 to house forestry staff.

REFRESHMENTS:

There are several pubs and cafés in Thornton Dale.

Walk 12 STAITHES – RUNSWICK BAY CIRCULAR 7m (11km)

Maps: OS Sheets Landranger 94; Outdoor Leisure 27.

Magnificent coastal scenery and country walking. A superb exploration of Captain Cook country.

Start: Staithes car park.

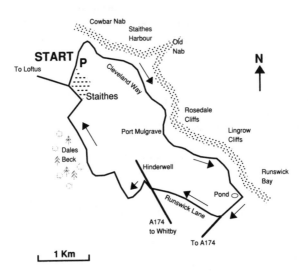

From Staithes car park go down Staithes Lane to the harbour where, just beyond the Cod and Lobster, turn right, up Church Street, passing **Captain Cook's Cottage**. At the top of the street climb steps and turn left at the Cleveland Way sign. Go up more steps and pass a farm on your right. Continue over two stiled fields and go diagonally uphill across the next one of the fenced cliff edge and at the hilltop cross a stile with a Cleveland Way signpost. The retrospective views from here reveal Boulby Cliffs, at 679 feet the highest in England. Continue southwards along a clear clifftop path and follow the Cleveland Way along Rosedale Lane to Port Mulgrave, a hamlet. Opposite No 79 Rosedale Lane go left along a path and over another stile near a Cleveland Way sign. Continue around Rosedale Cliffs and along the coast path for a further mile across the headland of High Lingrow and along Lingrow Cliffs, sometimes with a seaward

34

fence, sometimes without one, to a 'Runswick Bay' signpost. Turn right over a stile, go past a pond where a notice urges 'Help Protect Our Newts' and over another stile. Now follow a field path to the Runswick Bay Hotel on Runswick Bank Top. A short detour left down a 1 in 3 road will take you to the beautiful village of Runswick Bay.

The way forward is right, leaving the Cleveland Way, along Runswick Lane for 1 mile to Hinderwell and the A174, which you leave between Ivy Cottage and Jasmine Cottage. Do not be deceived by the signpost 'Footpath only to Doctor's Surgery' because this is a Right of Way to Back Lane via a housing estate, a school and a stiled field. Turn right into Back Lane and at its far end turn left over a stile and cross the field ahead to another stile. Cross this on to a waymarked footpath to Sylvan Borrowby Dale. Cross Dales Beck on a footbridge and go right, along a beckside path, climbing steadily through the woods. At a post with a yellow arrow choose the best of the paths ahead, the one that is by far the best defined, and continue across scrubland, crossing two stiles to follow a brick track to caravan sites. Now go over another stile, cross a plank bridge, fork right and aim for a gate marked 'No Through Road'. Take the path left of the gate, cross a railed fence above the caravan site and bear left, uphill, climbing steeply to cross a stile in the fence to the right of Seaton Hall. Cross the farm road, straddle the fence opposite and cross another field to the A174. Turn left along it and turn right along Staithes Lane to Staithes car park and the end of a delightful walk.

POINTS OF INTEREST:
Captain Cook's Cottage – Here there is a Heritage Trail Plaque which HRH The Prince of Wales unveiled on 1 June 1978. It says:
'The young James Cook received his taste of the sea and ships in this harbour village, where he worked as an assistant to William Sanderson, merchant, for 18 months, from 1745.'

REFRESHMENTS:
There are pubs in Staithes, Port Mulgrave and Runswick Bay.

Walk 13   ROBIN HOOD'S BAY   7m (11km)

Maps: OS Sheets Landranger 94; Outdoor Leisure 27.

A not too difficult walk giving excellent views of the beautiful Robin Hood's Bay. Part is muddy when wet.

Start: From either car park above Robin Hood's Bay village, or from the picnic area above the bay.

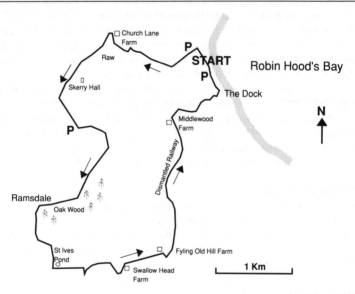

Walk past the left-hand side of the village hall and turn right, uphill, along the Scarborough road. Where the road turns left and levels, take the footpath on the right and continue uphill alongside Lingers Beck, crossing stiles to reach Church Lane. Turn left uphill and quickly right along a track after a house, 'Old Ridley'. Reach Raw Lane and turn left, through a gate ahead where the road bends. Keep the hedge on your right through two fields, and through a gate and a farmyard to reach Raw. Turn right and, immediately past a telephone box, turn left along a footpath. A small but interesting wet area is passed before a wider track is reached. Turn left and keep to the main track as it becomes more enclosed, and then keep on a narrow path close to the fence on your left as the field widens. Cross straight over a farm track and reach the Scarborough road just below the car park and picnic site. Turn left, downhill, and bear right at the junction, through a road gateway, to Fyling Hall School.

Opposite, a wide track goes steadily uphill by the side of, and through, woodland, before it bears left downhill to Ramsdale Mill Farm. Cross the bridge over Ramsdale Beck and walk uphill and through the left-hand gate into a field. The track continues ahead along the field side into Carr Wood. Turn left where the track reaches open fields by the side of St Ives pond. Pass through a gate and walk alongside the wall to a gate in the right-hand corner. Avoid mud with care and agility, and pass through a second gate to follow the track as it goes downhill bearing left towards gorse bushes and the left-hand side of Swallow Head Farm. Pass through, follow the farm road downhill and turn right to pass Fyling Old Hall. The road quickly bends left and a track goes off on the left to join the disused railway line.

Follow this tree-lined track through cuttings and over embankments. Reach a road, cross and rejoin the track. At Middlewood Farm cross the stile on your right, turn left to the field corner, and turn right along the field side. Bear left with this and, in a more open area, cross to the right, above the bushes, and cross a stile. The enclosed footpath joins a track and enters Robin Hood's Bay village (*see* Walk 9) along Albion Street. Turn left, uphill, to the car parks and the village hall.

REFRESHMENTS:

Plentiful in summer.

The Bay Hotel, near The Dock (tel no: 0947 880278).

The Victoria Hotel, near the car parks (tel no: 0947 880205).

Both provide meals at lunch and evening times throughout the year.

Walk 14   **RAVENSCAR**   7m (11km)

Maps: OS Sheets Landranger 94; Outdoor Leisure 27.

Disused railway line, farm road, and open moorland track provide variety with fairly easy walking. Some good views.

Start: Parking is usually easy on the road near the hotel in Ravenscar.

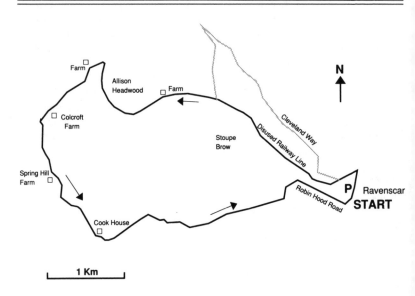

Take the track left before the hotel entrance and pass in front of the **National Trust Information Centre**. Soon bear left on to the disused railway line. The waymarked Cleveland Way can be used as a slightly longer and harder alternative start. The line passes by the disused Brickyard Alum Quarries, part of the National Trust Geological Trail, and rounds Stoupe Brow. If the Cleveland Way is used, turn left up the road reached to join the track via the left-hand side of the bridge. Pass under the bridge and continue past Browside Farm Pony Trekking Centre. The track now passes over a series of becks and through Allison Head Wood before being cut by the road near to Fyling Old Hall.

    A short track to the left leads to the road. Turn left, past the hall, and round the sharp bend to the right. Just before Fyling Old Hall Farm, and close to a small post box, a footpath bears left across grass and through a small gate. Maintain direction left, a little away from the fence, and then go downhill to a footbridge over a small beck. Jacob's Steps lead up from the beck to a road. Turn right and walk steadily uphill to reach Colcroft Farm on the left. A track bears left from the road, passing in front of an open, metal shed. Go downhill through woodland to a footbridge over a beck and continue uphill through a gate, going between the buildings of Spring Hill Farm. Slightly downhill, bear left over a small stream and through a gate. A little way uphill, in an open field, a grass track, bridleway signposted, bears left to reach a small gate. From here, a narrow, enclosed path leads to Cook House, between buildings, and to a farm road beyond.

Slightly to the left, take the main grass track bearing left, uphill, away from the concrete track. Open moorland is reached and soon the Ravenscar aerial is seen ahead. Scarborough Castle may be seen in the distance. The Lyke Wake Walk track crosses. Keep ahead and the two tracks soon merge, but a very wet area has to be avoided. Reach the road by the aerial and follow the footpath downhill by the fence and wall side, bearing right to join a track. Walk ahead and the track becomes Robin Hood Road. Turn left at the main road to return to the start.

POINTS OF INTEREST:
The National Trust Centre – This provides useful local information including details of the Geological Trail. Open at weekends and Bank Holidays during the summer. (10.30–1.30, 2.30–5 *or* 6).

REFRESHMENTS:
The Ravenscar Hall Hotel, Ravenscar (tel no: 0723 870353) supplies bar meals and has a restaurant.

Walk 15   **LEVISHAM BOTTOMS**   7$\frac{1}{2}$m (12km)

Maps: OS Sheets Landranger 94; Outdoor Leisure 27.

An easy moorland walk that combines legend, history and spectacular scenery.

Start: At Levisham.

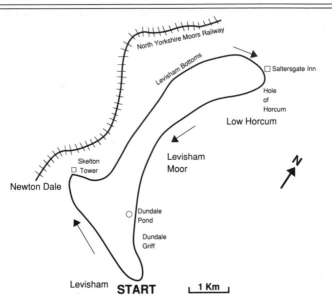

From Levisham go northwards, passing the Horseshoe Inn on your right and, ignoring the road to the station on your left, continue along Braygate Lane. After $\frac{1}{2}$ mile cross a signposted stile beside a gate which carries a notice, 'No unauthorised vehicles – keep dogs on lead', to enter **Levisham Moor**. Continue along a track to the right of a stone wall and where the wall ends keep straight ahead to descend West Side Brow on the moor's edge. Cross Levisham Bottoms to prominent **Skelton Tower** which overlooks the delightful Newton Dale. Continue north-easterly along a broad, moorland track for 1$\frac{1}{2}$ miles, with West Side Brow above and right and Newton Dale below and left.

Do not be tempted to turn right below the brow. Instead continue along the main track and leave the moor by crossing a stile beside a green, metal gate. Cross stepping stones, go half right over a rough pasture and over a couple of stiles to pass Glebe Farm

40

on your left. Now climb a stony track to the A169 and the **Saltersgate Inn**, a good mid-walk butty stop. From the pub go southwards along the road's verge – for easier walking – climbing to the hairpin bend known as the Devil's Elbow. Turn right near the top and cross a signposted stile near a gate marked 'No Model Flying or Hang Gliding Except Under Licence – Please Keep Dogs on Lead', to re-enter Levisham Moor. The views here are excellent both northwards to Fyling Dales and southwards into the famous **Hole of Horcum**, often called the Devil's Punch Bowl. Take the main moorland track south westerly passing Seavy Pond after 1 mile and continue in a more southerly direction for a further $1^1/_2$ miles to reach **Dundale Pond**. Continue up the track and leave the moor at a signposted stile, entering Limpsey Gate Lane. Follow this back to Levisham village.

POINTS OF INTEREST:

Levisham Moor – Seen at its best when purpled with heather. It is part of a 2,100 acre estate purchased by the National Park Authority in 1976.

Skelton Tower – Originally a shooting lodge, was built by Rev Robert Skelton, Rector of Levisham in the first part of the 19th century.

Saltersgate Inn – Situated on the old 'salt' road from Robin Hood's Bay to Saltersgate. Here smugglers brought their fish for salting in the days of the high salt tax. Prior to then it was an 18th century inn with its own toll bar and was called The Wagon and Horses.

The Hole of Horcum – So legend has it, was made by Giant Wade when he made Blakey Topping. It was from Horcum that he obtained the earth. Another legend credits the Devil with making the chasm into his Punch Bowl.

Dundale Pond – An informative sign here says: '*This small valley was given to the Monks of Malton Priory in about 1230 as a pasture for their sheep, cattle and horses. Dundale Pond was probably made at this time as a place for stock to drink*'.

REFRESHMENTS:

The Horseshoe Inn, Levisham (tel no: 0751 60240).
The Saltersgate Inn, (tel no: 0751 60237).

Walk 16　　　　　**WESTERDALE**　　　　　8m (13km)

Maps: OS Sheets Landranger 94; Outdoor Leisure 26.

Moderate walk, including moorland and farm tracks, on 1000 foot of climbing.

Start: At 665057, in Westerdale village.

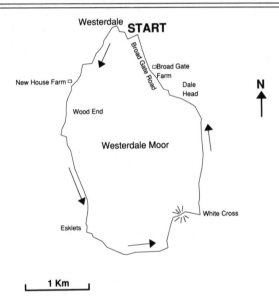

Take the lane which starts from the village street north of the church. Pass close to the Youth Hostel and Hall Farm, crossing the River Esk at a small wood. Continue uphill through two fields to the moor edge. Pass through a gate and go south along the road to New House Farm. On a bend a hundred yards before the farm pass through a second gate on your left. Go down and cross the field to the gate opposite. Cross Stockdale Beck by footbridge and continue, crossing the wall via a stile. Cross into the next field via a stone stile to the left of a telegraph pole. At Wood End Farm take the gate, right, pass behind the farm, leave the yard through a gate and go over a stone stile. Go over a footbridge and through a field, turning left to cross another footbridge near a ford. Turn right, following the River Esk upstream through three fields. Continue on the path over moorland and into the dale head, keeping to the left of the River Esk for $^3/_4$ mile until a footbridge is reached. Cross and walk through two fields of rough pasture, passing through the site of the demolished **Esklets Farm**.

At the end of a small enclosed lane on the south side of the farm buildings turn left and follow the route of the Lyke Wake Walk uphill. Passing to the right of Esklets Crag the path reaches the hilltop and joins the Castleton to Hutton-le-Hole road at the **Margery Bradley stone**.

Turn left and follow the road. At the T-junction near **Ralphs Cross** turn right on to the Rosedale road. Continue for 200yds past the car park (alternative start point) on your right and turn left leaving the road at **White Cross**. Follow the bridle path northwards, then descend to rejoin the Castleton road. Continue north on the road for about 1 mile to the road junction (to Danby Dale). The footpath back to Westerdale starts on the left of the road and goes north-west to descend to Dale Head Farm. Pass to the left of the farm and cross two fields keeping the wall on your left. Cross Tower Beck via a footbridge and follow the track passing Broad Gate Farm, to reach a farm road that leads back to the village.

POINTS OF INTEREST:

Esklets Farm – This abandoned farm was probably the oldest inhabited site in Westerdale, standing on the site of the shepherd's lodge erected by the Monks of Rievaulx when the Brus Lords od Skelton gave them rights of sheep pasture. The Monks were supported by armed lay brothers whose prime task was to protect the flocks from wolves.

Margery Bradley stone – A Neolithic standing stone that was, in the 17th century, called 'Broadless' which is a place where vagrants and beggars assembled to seek alms.

Moorland Crosses – More than twenty stone crosses are to be found on the North York Moors, often along ancient routes, many erected by the religious houses in medieval times. They may also have been used to mark crossroads and junctions of trackways. Old Ralph (674020) was mentioned as 'Crucem Radulphi' in the Guisborough Priory Charters of 1200. Another Ralphs Cross (Young Ralph) is at (677022). White Cross is also known as Fat Betty.

REFRESHMENTS:

The Lion Inn, Blakey Ridge (tel no: 07515 320).
Ryedale Folk Museum, Hutton-le-Hole (tel no: 07515 367).

Walk 17   **HUNMANBY**   8m (13km)

Maps: OS Sheets Landranger 101; Pathfinder TA 07/17.
Field tracks and paths with gently sloping hills partly along the Wolds Way. Pleasant views. Can be a little muddy underfoot.
Start: Opposite All Saints Church in Hunmanby.

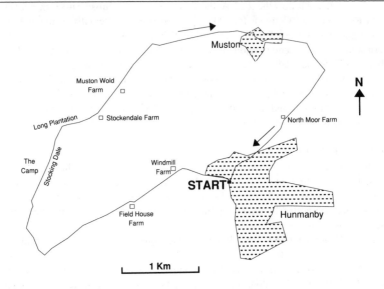

Walk uphill from the church and continue along Castle Hill straight across the Muston and Burton Fleming road junctions. Take a farm track on the left through Windmill Farm. At Field House Farm, turn right and quickly left along the wide track. This passes between fields to a gate at a T-junction. Turn right downhill. Bear right at the bottom along the field edge, with a fence on your right. The path should turn nearer to the centre of the dale in the more open area reached, but take the clearest path up to the junction with the Wolds Way as you bear right into Stocking Dale. Little remains of The Camp on the hill top to your left, a deserted village.

    The path goes clearly through some woodland ahead. Pass through a gate and continue up the dale to reach Long Plantation. Steadily turn right just before this to join a track going north-east to Stockendale Farm and a road. Cross and go through a gate opposite. The track goes by field sides and soon starts to descend off the edge of the Wolds. There are good views of the area towards Scarborough from here. Shortly after passing the second field boundary on your left, watch for a stile on your right which may be hidden in the hedge.

Cross the stile and bear left across the field to a fence corner. Enter the next field with a hedge on your left. Continue straight ahead downhill through several fields to reach a stile on to the A1039. This road is not usually very busy, but take care as you turn right and walk into **Muston**. Use the left-hand footpath, and just before a sharp bend left, and after the Ship Inn is passed, a footpath takes you to All Saints Church and back to the road. Continue along the footpath and, when the Wolds Way goes off to the left after a 'No Through Road', cross over to the right-hand footpath and turn right along the busier A165. Continue to the junction to Filey.

On the right-hand side here, pass through the left-hand gate on to a track. This takes you nearly south-westerly to the left-hand side of North Moor Farm. Here there are slight left and right bends in the track. Continue ahead through an enclosed track to reach **Hunmanby** on Northgate near a corner in the road. Go right and return to Castle Hill and the church.

POINTS OF INTEREST:
Munston – A quiet and fairly interesting village.
Hunmanby – A bustling village. There is a small craft shop along the road to the left down Bridlington Street. You will have passed Ye Old Coffee shop café by Castle Hill and there are a variety of pubs and fish and chip shops near to the church.

REFRESHMENTS:
The Ship Inn, Munston (tel no: 0723 512722).
Several in Hunmanby.

Walk 18   **BASIN HOWE**   8m (13km)

Maps: OS Sheets Landranger 101; Outdoor Leisure 27.

Fairly easy walking along footpaths and tracks largely through woodland. Good views of Troutsdale. Fairly good underfoot.

Start: From the parking area on the Snainton–Troutsdale road just above Troutsdale.

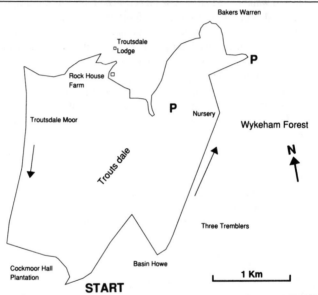

Take the track to the east by the side of woodland. **Basin Howe** Farm is across the field with the howe in front. Turn right along a narrow grass track just before a line of trees and reach a road. Turn right for a few yards to a forest track on your left. Continue ahead through a gate ignoring other tracks. Just before reaching a large nursery, a track joins from the right and the small **Three Tremblers** howes can be found. Immediately after the nursery, turn left along the path by the side of trees and reach a road. Turn right and, before long, the picnic area overlooking Troutsdale is reached.

    Turn left down the bridleway/ road. Take the first track off to the left, part way down the hill. A junction is reached and, less clear, two grass tracks descend from the gateposts on your right. Keep left. The track bears left and then right and between trees.

Immediately on reaching the open area here, turn left and take the path, not clear at first, along the side of, then through, trees to reach a footbridge over Troutsdale Beck. Follow the left-hand hedge up to a gate on the right and continue to the road, emerging by a small disused chapel. Turn left and uphill past Troutsdale Lodge and turn right at the corner into Rock House farmyard.

Take the first gate on your left and follow the slightly sunken track as it bears left to a gate. Continue up along the left-hand side of the hedge going through a gate into the wood. Take the right-hand path uphill to emerge on to moorland and walk along a very narrow path through heather straight across the moor generally aiming towards the edge of the group of trees ahead. Bear left along a clear drive through the trees to reach a wide track. Turn left. Do not use the smaller track. Pass by a more open area and continue ahead at a junction as the track becomes narrower and goes downhill. Keep left at a junction and walk down by the side of trees to reach a small gate. Go straight ahead through a field to reach a minor road. Turn left and walk to the Snainton road junction. Turn right uphill to the car park.

POINTS OF INTEREST:

Basin Howe – A fairly large example of a howe, or burial mound. Unfortunately it cannot be visited. There are many other earthworks in the area, particularly around the car park.

The Three Tremblers – These are much smaller, and well hidden by vegetation. They can be inspected though not much is visible.

REFRESHMENTS:

A farm on the Snainton road serves coffee and in Snainton there is a fish and chip shop. Meals can also be obtained from the Peacock Inn.

Walk 19   **DANBY & COMMONDALE**   8m (13km)

Maps: OS Sheets Landranger 94; Outdoor Leisure 26.

Moderate walk, including moorland, and farm tracks. Total climbing over the whole route 240m.

Start: At 709087, in the layby adjacent to the post office, Danby.

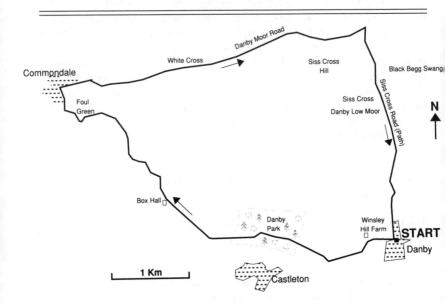

From the car park go past the post office, cross straight over the crossroads at the Duke of Wellington pub and follow the minor road towards Castleton for about ¹/₂ mile, until the access road to Winsley Hill farm is reached. Shortly after this point the road begins to drop towards the River Esk. Take the bridle path which forks right and continue across open moorland for about ¹/₂ mile until Danby Park, a birch wood, is reached.

Pass through the gate and continue through the wood. The path passes Park Nook Farm and some cottages, and then joins the Castleton to Lockwood Beck road halfway up the bank above the railway station.

Climb the bank and at the top where the road bends sharply to the right, take the farm road ahead of you which descends into the valley above the railway line. This farm road passes the farms of Box Hall and Cobble Hall, then goes through another birch

48

wood, leading through a gate on to a lane joining the road opposite Foul Green Farm. Follow the road towards Commondale: it runs parallel with the trackbed of the railway sidings which served the long demolished brickworks. After a short walk the centre of Commondale village is reached, many of the houses being built of local brick.

Immediately before the T-junction is reached, turn right opposite the Cleveland Inn car park and cross the small green. Keep to the right-hand side and walk uphill following the **Flagged Causeway**, passing to the right of the old school. Cross two small grassy fields by stiles, reaching the moor edge via a gate. The causeway veers to the right and keeps to the left of a drystone wall. It can be followed for a few hundred yards until it reaches the road.

Turn right and follow the road to the T-junction at **White Cross**. From there continue ahead on the unsurfaced road named 'Danby Moor Road' for about $1^1/_2$ miles. (Some of this can be very boggy.) At a point marked by a public bridleway sign, turn right and follow the track named 'Siss Cross Road' which climbs gently in a southerly direction passing to the left of Siss Cross on Danby Low Moor.

The path then descends to join the road to Danby at a point above a Z-bend above the village. Take the path which cuts the corner off the bend and rejoin the road which drops steeply into the village and back to the start point.

POINTS OF INTEREST:

Flagged Causeway – The causeway leading out of Commondale village is typical of those to be found on the North York Moors. Many of the routes can be traced back to medieval times and may have been pioneered by monks on the routes between abbeys and granges. These causeways were at one time the only means of communication across the moors.

White Cross – This cross, at 679108, marks the place where the ancient Stokesley to Whitby road crossed the Castleton Road.

REFRESHMENTS:

The Duke of Wellington, Danby (tel no: 0287 60351).
The Cleveland Inn, Commondale (tel no: 0287 60214).

Walk 20   FORGE VALLEY AND SCALBY   8m (13km)

Maps: OS Sheets Landranger 101; Outdoor Leisure 27.

Generally flat walking on fairly good paths and tracks, part stream side. Muddy near the end.

Start: At the picnic site off the Hackness road just north of the road junction at the northern end of Forge Valley.

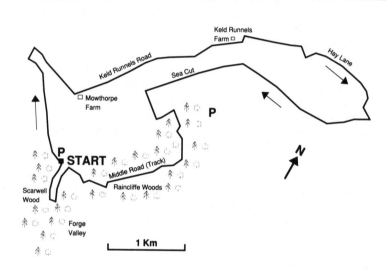

A footpath passes through the trees at the south-western corner of the site and leads to the road through the valley. Pass quietly by an area where food left attracts many birds and squirrels. A path soon leads down to a bridge over the River Derwent. Cross and turn right. Follow the riverside path, much on wooden boards, to a stile. Cross and bear left up a slight hill, taking care in this often wet area, then bear right alongside the trees. A clear track to a gate is reached. Pass through and follow the embankment to a stile on your right. Cross and bear left to another stile and, a little to the right, a third. Continue to the junction of the Derwent with the **Sea Cut**.

    Turn right along the latter and reach Mowthorp bridge. Cross and turn right through a farmyard and a gate. Take the wide track, Keld Runnels Road, uphill and continue ahead where it enters Holly Wood. Beyond, it descends slightly and soon widens as it passes a farm. The track eventually meets a road at Hay Brow. Cross to the footpath and walk down the road to Scalby. To see the village, continue past the church ahead, and perhaps visit a tea shop further along. Otherwise turn right at the road junction and once again reach Sea Cut.

Cross the bridge and turn right along the streamside. Just before the end of the last field on the opposite bank, and before some bushes on the embankment side, look for a stile and footbridge below. Cross and aim to the right of a group of trees across the field to reach a track, often muddy. Turn left at the end along a bridleway. Go through the centre gate, pass through another gate and turn right before the next gateway to reach the road. Turn right and, before the dip in the road, turn left along a track uphill into Rainscliffe Woods. Ignore other paths until a wide, stone surfaced track (Middle Road) is reached. Turn right and keep to the left as a sawmill is past. The track descends to reach the road close to the junction near the **Forge Valley** picnic site.

POINTS OF INTEREST:
Sea Cut – This man-made stream helps prevent flooding by taking overflow from the Derwent to the sea via Scalby Beck.
Forge Valley – The River Derwent cuts through this lovely valley on its long journey to the sea via the Humber. The Nature Conservancy Council help to maintain its rich flora and fauna, particularly the wetland plants. Look out for rare species of birds. Different species of tits and herons are common, and kingfishers are present along the river and Sea Cut.

REFRESHMENTS:
No refreshments are available in the valley area but are plentiful nearby in East Ayton, Scalby, Seamer and Scarborough.

Walk 21   BAYSDALE AND WESTERDALE   8m (13km)

Maps: OS Sheets Landranger 94; Outdoor Leisure 26.

Moorland, farm tracks and arable land. About 800 feet of climbing.

Start: At 685084, in the car park by Castleton railway station.

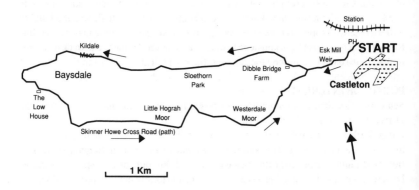

Take the road signposted **Westerdale** and follow it, passing the Esk Mill, until a crossroads is reached. Turn right, downhill to cross the River Esk via Dibble Bridge and continue uphill passing the T-junction to Commondale. Continue on the minor road, passing through the fields of Haggaback Farm, crossing open moorland and then descending to join the Westerdale to Kildale road at a T-junction. A bridle path starts here and contours west along the north side of Baysdale for about 1¹/₂ miles to a ruined farm. Pass the first building, then bear left through a gate following the track past the front of the farmhouse. The track descends into the valley and goes through a gate hole in a wall to the left of a stone barn. Cross Baysdale Beck via a cart bridge and turn immediately left after passing a modern barn. Follow the farm lane uphill to the buildings of the Low House. Enter the yard, go through the gate on the left of the house and continue uphill on a broad track to the edge of a plantation. The path crosses open moorland and descends into Great Hograh, crossing the beck via a stone bridge. Continue along the path (Skinner Howe Cross Road) which is waymarked at intervals with stone cairns. After about $1^1/_2$ miles of moorland walking the path ends at a minor road.

Turn left and follow the road for a $^1/_4$ mile to join the Kildale to Westerdale road. Go right for about two hundred yards. An indistinct footpath forks left from this point, near the brow of the hill.

Follow the path south-east and downhill to Dale View Farm. Pass the farm and continue, then turn right, passing through two gates, then left towards a small wood, passing a hay shed on the left. Pass through the first field gate and go to the bottom corner of the wood. From the corner turn left for a few yards and then right, crossing the wall by stone steps. Continue with the wall now on your right, the path descending into the valley. Cross the river Esk by footbridge and turn left uphill to the corner of a field. The path now follows the river bank until it reaches Dibble Bridge. Turn right at the bridge and walk uphill on the road. Go left at the crossroads, descending into the valley, passing the cricket field to reach the start.

POINTS OF INTEREST:

Westerdale – At the south east corner of the main street is a cottage named 'Arkangel'. A curious stone monument in the garden was erected by Thomas Bulmer, an old sailor. The lettering around the shaft relates to the many countries he had visited on his voyages and how he survived a shipwreck in 1729.

REFRESHMENTS:

The Eskdale Hotel, Castleton (tel no: 0287 60234).
The Danby Lodge Moors Centre, (tel no: 0287 60540).

Walk 22 GLAISDALE 8m (13km)

Maps: OS Sheets Landranger 94; Outdoor Leisure 27.

An upland moor ramble with some easy climbing.

Start: At 784055, Beggars Bridge, Glaisdale.

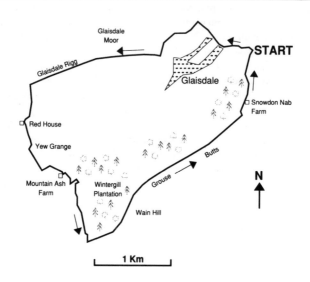

Walk up the hill past the Railway Station into the centre of the village. Continue on the main road through the village to **The Green**. Turn left and follow the road until a gate is reached. Go through the gate to reach open moorland, the tarmac road giving way to a wide stony track known as Glaisdale Rigg. After about 150 yards turn on to a tractor track on your left following a wire fence and then a wall. When the wall turns sharp left notice a memorial stone (dedicated to the former owners of Hall Farm) set into the wall. The view from this point is the reason for the diversion from the Rigg. Return to the Rigg by a path on your right, ignoring the Public Bridleway sign in front of the path. Continue along Glaisdale Rigg in a westerly direction, ignoring all tracks leading from it. After about 2 miles an unfenced moorland road appears: our route heads off about twenty yards before the road is reached. A metal post to the right bearing a notice 'Unsuitable for Motors' indicates the point where we leave the Rigg. Head left here and descend the moor. On reaching some brick manholes cross them and head slightly right across the moor to descend to a stone wall. On reaching the stone wall turn left, passing the ruins of Red House to arrive at a wall corner. Pass through the gate and follow the Wall on your right to another gate. Now, with the wall on your left, go down to the gate which leads into a quiet country lane. Turn left and then almost immediately right to pass over a bridge. Follow the road past Yew Grange Farm and the picturesque Hob Garth until you reach Mountain Ash Farm and as the road swings round the back of the farm, a Public Bridleway sign will be seen on your right. Go through the metal gate and climb up the middle of the field to another metal gate, taking the right-hand path once through the gate. The path runs in a gully up to a stone wall and iron gate from where it heads in a southerly direction towards trees in the middle distance. Head towards the trees, but before reaching them the track turns left up the moor towards a gate in a stone wall. Pass through the gate to follow the track slightly right (south), again running in a gully. Follow the path right across the moor to reach an unfenced moorland road. Turn left. There now follows a high-level road walk for three miles, but the road is quiet and the views are extensive. Once the road becomes enclosed, after a cattle grid, it starts to descend. After about $1/_2$ mile a tarmacked lane appears on your left. Turn down this and follow it to its end, where it changes to a green track. Follow the green track through the woods to arrive back at Beggars Bridge.

POINTS OF INTEREST:

The Green – Despite being marked on the map as The Green it is not typical of village greens in this area, rather a triangular shaped area of grass.

REFRESHMENTS:

The Anglers Rest Inn, Glaisdale (tel no: 0947 87261).
The Arncliffe Arms, Glaisdale (tel no: 0947 87209).
The Mitre Tavern, Glaisdale (tel no: 0947 87315).

Walk 23   **FARNDALE**   8m (14km)

Maps: OS Sheets Landranger 94; Outdoor Leisure 26.

Moderate walk, including moorland, arable and farm tracks, and waterside paths. About 750 feet of climbing.

Start: At 659927, near Rudland Rigg. During the daffodil season it may be necessary to use the Low Mill car park at 673952.

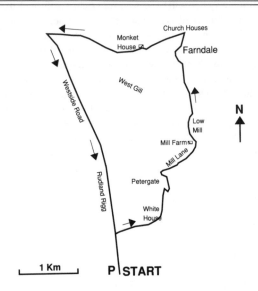

Follow the unsurfaced county road northwards on to Rudland Rigg. This road is one of the old major roads across the moors going north to Ingleby Greenhow near Stokesley. It is still a public road, but only for suitable vehicles!

    After a gradual climb of about $^1/_2$ mile, turn right on a track to White House Farm. The track forks at the farm buildings. Take the left fork across $^1/_2$ mile of moorland to old quarries. Here take a footpath down to the road in Farndale. Follow the road into Low Mill and take the left fork which is signposted Farndale Eastside. After a hundred yards you will see an obvious signed footpath leading down to the River Dove. If you are only out to see the daffodils this is where the car park is, and where the crowds start. It is worth mentioning that as these daffodils are wild they are several weeks behind garden ones, and even after a mild winter they are seldom worth seeing before April 1st.

There is little point explaining the route from here to Church Houses, it's a well-defined well-surfaced footpath crossing several footbridges and going through woodland to High Mill. From there it becomes a farm track to the Feversham Arms at Church Houses. From Church Houses take the road to the left leading uphill to a T-junction where you turn right to Monket House. Straight in front of the house is a gate on your left. Go through this gate and follow the track uphill via the crags on to Rudland Rigg. In wet weather this track is very slippery at those places where it is worn through to the shale. The track is another unsurfaced county highway leading to Bransdale, which you follow for a mile to join the main track on Rudland Rigg. Once you join the main track turn left and climb slightly for a mile to reach the os triangulation pillar on your right. In autumn this whole section across Rudland Rigg will be awash with the purple flowering of the ling (heather to the layman) as will almost everything that you can see to the west, north and east. Southwards, ahead, you will see arable land and forestry stretching towards the tabular hills at the southern edge of the National Park.

A further walk of $1^1/_2$ miles will have you back at your vehicle.

POINTS OF INTEREST:
To check with a National Park office about the daffodils, ring the Danby Moors Centre (0287 60540) or Sutton Bank Information Centre (0845 597426).

REFRESHMENTS:
Ryedale Folk Museum, Hutton-le-Hole (tel no: 0751 5367).
The Feversham Arms, Farndale (tel no: 0751 33206).
The Lion Inn, Blakey (tel no: 0751 5320).
And for real ale enthusiasts try:
The New Inn, at Cropton, where they brew their own (tel no: 0751 5330).

Walk 24   **FILEY**   9m (14.5km)

Maps: OS Sheets Landranger 101; Pathfinder TA 08/18 & 07/17.
A slightly strenuous walk along field paths, tracks, roads, and clifftop needing some care. Part may be muddy underfoot.
Start: By the bus station in Filey.

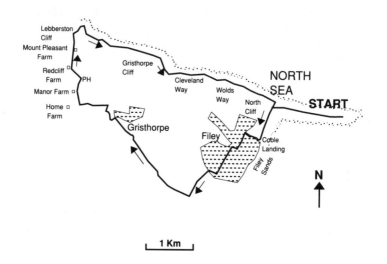

Take the A1039 Bridlington road. Near a school, turn right along the Wolds Way track and left over a footbridge at the field corner. Continue ahead to reach the A165. Carefully cross to the stile opposite. Follow the field edge to a stile on your left. Cross and walk right to a small gate and Muston (*see* Walk 17). Turn right into a lane which turns into a rough track. Some gates may be better climbed along here!

Keep right at a footpath junction and take the left of two gates. The track becomes a field edge path maintaining the same direction. Pass through a rough barricade of gates on your right and turn left over gates and stiles ahead to reach some trees. Turn right and cross the footbridge on your left to reach the railway gates. Check before crossing. Bear slightly left to a gate and track which leads through a farmyard to Gristhorpe, a pleasant village. Turn left along the road and, as it bends, use the bridleway, right, to reach a quiet road. Turn left to Lebberston. The road bears right near to the Ox Inn. Cross the B1261 Cayton road and continue to the roundabout on the A165 Scarborough road by the Plough Inn. Cross on the right and take the old road behind the Inn. Before Redcliffe Farm, a track goes uphill past Mount Pleasant Farm. Unfasten wires (if necessary) across a gateway before using the left-hand side of a field to reach the clifftop and the Cleveland Way.

Take care: the cliff path is a little eroded in parts. Turn right to follow it back to **Filey**. You will pass a caravan site and eventually reach a wooden fence. Note the look-out post: the Cleveland Way meets Wolds Way here on **Carr Naze**. A path down on your right gives access to **Filey Brigg**.

Continue along clifftop or beach past the Country Park and the Yacht Club. The **Coble Landing** beyond is worth seeing. Take the path up to the right of the ravine to St Oswald's Church and go left over the bridge. You will pass some interesting old cottages on your way: go straight ahead across junctions to reach a roundabout and the bus station.

POINTS OF INTEREST:

Filey – A fairly quiet resort with excellent sands.

Carr Naze – Had a Roman signal station. The Cleveland and Wolds Ways meet here.

Filey Brigg – Said to have been built by the Devil, or to be the bones of a long dead dragon. The rocks of the Brigg extend well out to sea and are worth exploring with care at low tide. Bird migration provides rewarding watching.

Coble Landing – Has gaily painted fishing cobles and sea food stalls.

REFRESHMENTS:

Refreshment can be obtained from a variety of cafés and pubs in Filey, though there are fewer open in the winter.

Walk 25   **WINTRINGHAM**   9m (14.5km)

Maps: OS Sheets Landranger 100 & 101; Pathfinder SE 87/97 & 86/96.

A moderately hilly walk on the northern edge of the Wolds using field paths and tracks. Excellent views. Fairly good underfoot.
Start: In Wintringham.

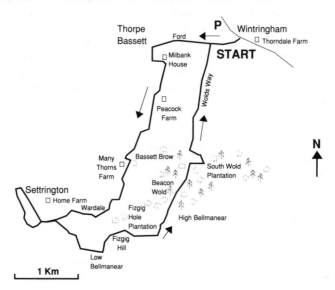

Leave **Wintringham** along the Wolds Way from opposite Thorndale Farm. Cross the footbridge over Wintringham Beck and cross the field ahead to a small gate. Follow the field edge to reach a farm road. Take the bridleway slightly to the right along a field edge to reach a small gate and gap on the right and change to the opposite side of the hedge. Go along a track to Thorpe Bassett. Turn left along the village road and left again along a road just after passing a telephone box. The road bears right. Shortly, turn right at a footpath just before a holly bush, cross a bridge and enter a field. Turn left and follow the field edge past Peacock Farm, through a gate, over a stile and, still with the field edge on your left, reach a small building. Pass this and turn right soon, with a small drain on your left, to reach a stile. Cross and turn left to another stile. Bear right, uphill, to the side of the plantation on your right to reach a gate and the remains of Many Thorns Farm.

From the track behind, follow the right-hand side of the hedge going uphill. Cross a stile and bear right towards a telegraph pole. Cross a road and take the track to Wold House. Bear right to a stile just before the farm, cross a stile and walk downhill through a gap in the bushes and reach a gate in the bottom right-hand corner of the field. Bear right to a stile and gateway in the field corner. Cross with care, turn left and, after passing through a line of bushes, bear right, uphill to reach a gate and a track in the top right corner. Follow the track past Wardale Farm. Turn left at the road.

On the left, just before a line of trees, a track goes to Low Bellmanear Farm, but you may wish to explore **Settrington**, on the road ahead, first. The track bears right and then left by the side of a plantation to reach the farm. Turn left in front of it, across a bridge, and follow the fairly clear track as it bears slightly right, through a gate. Keep right, uphill, to the left-hand side of a plantation on Fizgig Hill. Go through, or over the gate, cross a stile, and walk along the field edge to reach a track. This is the Wolds Way again. Turn left and follow the track past High Bellmanear Farm to a road close to the hidden Settrington Beacon. Cross to the forest track. Turn right at a T-junction and soon turn left where the track bends right. The narrow path reaches a gate from where a wide track descends. Turn right at the fence and follow the track, which becomes a tarmacked road, keeping right at a junction, to reach the path used earlier. Retrace your steps to Wintringham.

POINTS OF INTEREST:

Wintringham – A small village with white painted cottages. Its large church has an interesting warning for bell ringers.

Settrington – A larger village with interesting buildings including its ancient church. A stream runs through the village.

REFRESHMENTS:

Just one shop in Settrington. Nearby Rillington has two inns and a café as well as shops.

Walk 26   **REASTY BANK AND HACKNESS**   9m (14.5km)
Maps: OS Sheets Landranger 101; Outdoor Leisure 27.
Slightly hilly walking, much through forest, and with some pleasant views.
Start: At 965945, the car park at the top of Reasty Bank.

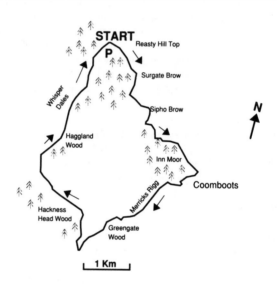

From the north-east corner of the car park take the right-hand track through woodland. Ignore all junctions and keep to the wide track overlooking Surgate Brow. When the road from Burniston is reached, turn right and then left at a junction before re-entering the woodland on your left. Continue to walk along the brow of the hill. Twice the route returns to the road before finally reaching it again at Coomboots Brow. Take the footpath on the opposite side of the road, with the fence on your right, until it bears left. Pass through here to follow the other side, soon going downhill through the centre of a wooded valley. Go through a gate and a field to reach the road near Hackness. Turn right, and soon bear left off the road, going slightly uphill along the edge of the trees to reach a stile. Cross and walk uphill on a clear path. From here there are excellent views of **Hackness Hall** and lake.

Just before reaching the tree-line, the path descends to meet the edge of the trees at a corner. Descending too early can cause problems mounting the haha. Bear left a little below the tree-line to a stile. Go over to reach a steeper downhill slope and cross a stile to the road. Turn right along the road and again right at the junction, with Hackness lake on your right. Immediately before a bridge, turn left along the narrow road to Highdales. Cross a footbridge at the ford and enter a field on the right of the track. Maintain your direction to reach a gate at the left-hand side of Lowdales farm. Turn right between the buildings and continue along the wide track. This passes the end of a valley on your right and is less clear through a small, gated field as it enters Whisper Dales. The track passes to the opposite side of the stream and Whisperdales farm on your left. Pass through a gate and take the track as it rises fairly gently uphill into the forest on the right-hand side of the centre of three valleys. Keep on this main track as it bears right at a junction to bring you back to **Reasty Bank**.

POINTS OF INTEREST:

Hackness Hall – Is in a beautiful setting. It is the home of Lord Derwent who has been very helpful to walkers in the past. Herons are amongst the birds often seen on the lake.
Reasty Bank – There is plenty of parking space at this popular picnic site. A Silpho Forest trail starts here as well as the Pickering Forest 'Blue Man' walk to Allerston.

REFRESHMENTS:

Cannot be obtained along the route but plenty are available in the area particularly in Scarborough. Drive down through Harewood Dale and turn right along the Scarborough road to reach the Flask Inn which serves walkers well.

Walk 27   REASTY BANK AND LANGDALE END   9m (14.5km)

Maps: OS Sheets Landranger 101; Outdoor Leisure 27.

Some forest walking with pleasant views. A little hilly.

Start: At 965945, the car park at the top of Reasty Bank.

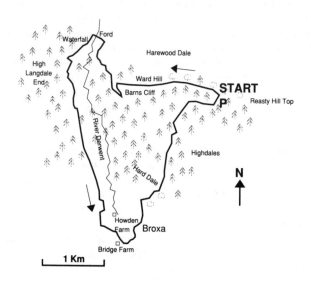

From the car park take the wide track leading westerly on top of the hill, overlooking Harewood Dale. Just after the track turns south, at Barns Cliff above Langdale, a footpath on the right descends to the valley. At first it goes almost due north through trees, but then bears a little to the left. At a junction, maintain height just inside the tree-line to reach a path that descends fairly directly just round to the northern edge of the hill. When the river is reached, turn towards the bottom of the hill corner and find a footbridge over the beck. Follow the path ahead which goes uphill by the side of trees and then turn left, keeping to the edge of the trees until a track down to the River Derwent is reached. Take care in this motorcycle racing area. Ford the river, or if too wet go to the footbridge just downstream and return along the rough path on the opposite bank.

    Follow the track which becomes only a path as it passes to the right of High

Langdale End farm. At the track junction ahead turn left, then right and left again to climb along the western side of Langdale Rigg End. The track runs southerly by the edge of trees before turning sharp left. Shortly, turn right off this track to follow a wide footpath through the forest and along the top of Langdale Rigg. This emerges into open land and bears left as it descends the end of the rigg. Go through a gate into a field, then through another gate in the right-hand corner to reach the road. There are good views of isolated Howden Hill, but beware of adders in warm weather!

Turn left along the road, then left at the junction to reach **Langdale End**. Cross Langdale Bridge and take the footpath on your left uphill by the side of trees to join the bridleway and the road to Broxa. Pass two fields after the hamlet and then follow the path, right, with a fence on your right, to shortly descend through a small wooded valley to a gate. Cross the field beyond to a gate near to the side of Highdales Beck and follow the side of the beck up High Dales until you reach a building on the opposite side of the beck. Here cross a stile and the beck. Turn left along the track and immediately pass through a gate on the right and follow the wide path uphill and into the forest. This can be muddy! At a corner bear right, keeping to the obvious main track up to a T-junction. Turn left and follow the track as it bears right by the side of a more open area, and continues easterly. Turn left at the next junction to quickly arrive back at Reasty Bank Top.

POINTS OF INTEREST:

Langdale End – Has a post office. Refreshment may be available: the unusual Inn, which had a six day licence has recently changed hands and its future was a little uncertain at the time of writing.

Walk 28   HUTTON-LE-HOLE   9m (14.5km)

Maps: OS Sheets Landranger 94 or 100, Outdoor Leisure 27.

A fine, moorland walk with some road walking and one steep climb.

Start: The car park, Hutton-le-Hole.

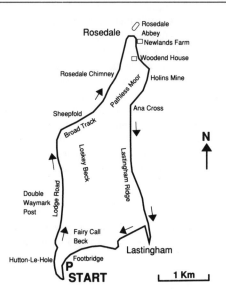

From the car park go right along Moor Lane and where it bends right, go left along a signposted moorland path, climbing steadily. After about 1 mile join Lodge Road, a moorland track, and continue along it for $^1/_4$ mile to a double waymarked post where Lodge Road turns left. Continue north on the moorland path ahead for a mile to join an intersecting track. A large post marked 'Footpath' and with a white arrow, points the way, right (east), along a broad track , for about $^1/_2$ mile. The track drops to cross Loskey Beck and climbs again. Where it bends right, leave it and go straight ahead, passing a sheepfold on your right. Cross a stream and go half left and up on a broadening track to reach the Rosedale road. Go left, north along this road, with extensive views including the 'Golf Balls' of Fylingdales. The top of **Rosedale Chimney** Bank, with its good views over Rosedale, makes a good butty stop. The moorland track on your right will take you directly to Anna Cross. It is well used by hikers but is not shown as a right of way on the map. The correct way for this walk is to continue along the road going steeply down to the White Horse Farm Hotel. Go right here along a signposted bridleway past Newlands Farm and, further on, Woodend House. Once past a red roofed barn on your left watch for a sheep dip and go through an unmarked gate opposite it. Bear half left up the hillside and left again to go through a gate marked 'Please Shut This Gate' into disused **Hollins Mine**. Continue straight ahead across the spoil heaps, then turn right up a steep hillside path indicated by a white painted stone. The way here is a bit rough between more spoil heaps to the top where the moor ahead is pathless. Bear half-left across heather aiming for **Anna Cross**, a good landmark. From Anna Cross the way is south over Spaunton Moor along a broad, cairned track for 2 miles into Lastingham. This lovely village must be visited, so, as you approach it, note a triple footpath sign at the edge of the moor. It is to here that you return after visiting **St Mary's Church** and the Blacksmith's Arms. From the sign go left, westwards, along the edge of the moor, close to the moor wall, and descend to, and cross, Hole Beck. Climb up to pass, to the left, Camomile Farm. The track leaves the moor, left, along the lane to reach Moor Lane. Go right for $^1/_2$ mile. At a double footpath sign fork left on the downhill path. Go through woodland and over Fairy Call Beck into fields. Go south-west along a waymarked route over four fields. Pass St Chad's Church, turn left by the bowling green and go along an enclosed path to exit opposite the Village Hall close to the start.

POINTS OF INTEREST:

The Rosedale Chimney – Once a popular landmark stood at the top of Rosedale Chimney Bank until it was demolished on July 27th, 1972.

Hollins Mine – Was an important iron mine, opened in 1856 and closed in 1885.

Anna Cross – The original can be seen in Lastingham Church. The one on Spaunton Moor is an 18th or 19th Century replica. Also known as the Anna Ain Howe Cross.

St Mary's Church – The ancient crypt was built in 1078 on the site of a Celtic monastery and is the shrine of St Cedd who brought Christianity to this part of England.

REFRESHMENTS:

The Crown, Hutton-le-Hole (tel no: 07515 343).

The White Horse Farm Hotel, Rosedale Abbey (tel no: 07515 239).

The Blacksmith's Arms, Lastingham (tel no: 07515 247).

There are tea rooms in Hutton-le-Hole and a restaurant in Lastingham.

Walk 29   **K**ILDALE TO **R**OSEBERRY **T**OPPING   9$\frac{1}{2}$m (15km)
Maps: OS Sheets Landranger 93 & 94; Outdoor Leisure 26.
A long, but moderate walk.
Start: At 605095, near the site of Kildale railway station. The
approach is a rough lane.

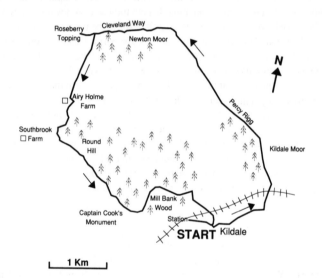

Walk back through the village and turn left along the road to Commondale and
Castleton. After $\frac{3}{4}$ mile, turn left at a letter box and go up the lane to New Row Cottages.
Keep straight on uphill on the track, passing the right-hand side of the wood. When you
reach the road over Percy Cross Rigg, turn left and walk along the road. Note the
remains of an Iron Age settlement on the right. The tarmac terminates at the end of the
wood: continue forward along a rough track with a view of the sea down to the right.
When you reach a gate, go through and turn left along the edge of the forest.

After $\frac{1}{2}$ mile the forest road turns right. Here, go forward through a wicket gate.
Roseberry Topping is in front of you, its odd shape partly due to quarrying. Follow a
distinct path forward through the heather to another wicket gate. Go through this and
continue down hill. If making a detour to the Topping, you should return to this point.

Go through the gate – on the left as you look towards the hill – and follow a field road to Airy Holme Farm. Bear left and pass in front of the farm. Continue down a tree-shaded lane to a crossroads near some cottages.

Go straight across and follow a tarmacked lane which finishes at a house called 'Nannybean'. The path continues as a rough, uphill track. Go through the gate at the top of the hill, continue by a stone wall and keep straight on by the left-hand side of a fence. On reaching the next gate, go straight across the forest road to follow a narrow path through the trees. Go along a bracken-covered hillside from which Captain Cook's Monument can be glimpsed up to the left, and, to the right, there is a good view of the Cleveland Hills. Mill Bank Woods is entered between stone gateposts. Keep straight forward on a forest track which can be muddy, to reach a stile and gate giving access to a road near Bankside Farm.

Follow the road downhill to Kildale village. Turn right on the road signposted 'Kildale Station only' and return to your start point.

Walk 30   **ROSEDALE IRONSTONE RAILWAY**   11m (17.5km)
Maps: OS Sheets Landranger 94; Outdoor Leisure 26.
A long, but straightforward and interesting route.
Start: At 720945, near the 'Steep Hill' notice at the top of the 1
in 3 Rosedale Chimney Bank.

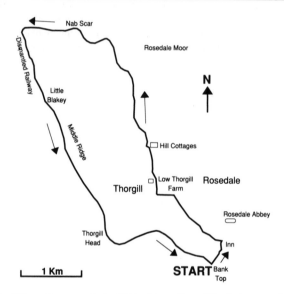

Walk down the hill until you reach the White Horse Farm Hotel, then turn left on the
road signposted 'Thorgill Only'. After 1 mile, just before a sharp left-hand bend, turn
right down a farm road to Low Thorgill Farm. The road passes between farm buildings
and then turns towards the farmhouse. Go through the gate on the right, where there is
a public footpath sign, and walk diagonally to the left to cross the River Seven by a
footbridge. Bear left along a paved trod, some of the stones buried in the soil, to reach
a distinct path going uphill to a gap in the hedge. Continue up by the hedge to a wide
track and a terrace of ironworker's cottages by a narrow road.

  Take the track immediately opposite, ascending to the site of the Rosedale
goods station and the ruins of the coal depot. The white-painted house was once the
'Depot Cottage'. At the top of the bank, go through a gate and past the left-hand side

of Low Baring – ruined cottages – to reach the railway track bed. Jackdaws haunt these old iron ore kilns.

From here the route is straightforward, the railway making an $8^1/_2$ mile loop round the head of **Rosedale**. There are beautiful views, and unusual flowers can be found in the ballast. The route of the 40 mile Lyke Wake Walk goes across the head of this valley. On the way back from the dalehead, a footpath up to the right leads to Blakey Ridge and the Lion Inn, should you need refreshment. On warm days, watch out for basking adders.

The railway track will bring you back to your starting point.

POINTS OF INTEREST:

Rosedale – Was once the centre of the local ironstone industry. Rolling stock from Middlesborough would be hauled up Ingleby Incline by steel ropes to the moor top. Production of ironstone ceased in 1926, the rails taken up, and the smelting chimney demolished. Nearby Rosedale Abbey is a picturesque village nestling at the foot of Chimney Bank. All that remains of the abbey of the name, founded in 1158, is a short tower and staircase near St Lawrence's church.

REFRESHMENTS:

The White Horse Farm Hotel, children and pets welcome (tel no: 0715 239).

Walks 31 and 32 **BOROUGHBRIDGE AND ALDBOROUGH** 5m (8km) and 8m (13km).

Maps: OS Sheets Landranger 99; Pathfinder SE 26/36 & 46/56.

A walk within historic Boroughbridge and nearby countryside , including a pleasant and interesting extension to Aldborough.

Start: The Market Cross in St James' Square, Boroughbridge.

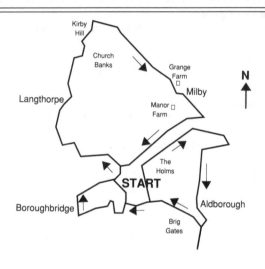

Cross to Church Lane and opposite St James' Church take the narrow lane to New Row. Turn right and soon left along St Helena, across the River Tutt. Bear left past the toilets and cross a little left to Roecliffe Lane. Turn right along the track to the timber firm. Take the footpath on the right, near a bungalow, to reach an estate road. Follow this left and as it then bears right to Chatsworth Grove. Turn left at the end, along Horsefair, and cross the bridge over the River Ure. Divert left into the picnic area to see the weir. Turn left at the roundabout, behind the petrol station, and follow the riverside path.

Pass through a fence and turn right along a path between houses to reach Skelton Road. Turn left, cross the road and turn right down the lane by The Gables, a little before an inn. Cross the low wall on the right, by the waymark, and turn left through the orchard to the caravan park. The footpath should pass between the 4th and 5th caravans by the northern hedge, but it may be necessary to divert to the right of the hedge in order to enter the next field. Cross this to the left-hand corner of the houses that are slightly to the right. A path here goes to Leeming Lane. Turn left. Cross to the start of the last field before the houses on the right, and bear left across this towards the right of the houses, walking a little uphill. Turn right along the hedge and turn left over a stile. Follow the hedge on the right and bear right at the corner to a kissing gate. Go through and continue to All Saints' Church at Kirby Hill.

Turn right to reach a cross roads. Turn right and quickly cross and bear left down the track to Milby. Cross the road here and pass a house on the left. Immediately turn left between houses and enter a field. Turn right along the edge and continue from the corner ahead between crops to the River Ure. Turn left and follow the riverside path. Go over a footbridge by Milby Lock and back to **Boroughbridge**. Turn left and return to the start.

To extend the walk take the road to Aldborough from the square. Just past the school, turn left along the wide track to the river. Turn right along the riverside. Cross two stiles to reach a larger open field. Turn right along the fence to the end of a track on the right. Follow this to **Aldborough**. Visit the nearby church, and from its southern exit walk ahead past the green to the Roman Town Museum. Return to the old cross near the church and turn left along the road to return to Boroughbridge.

POINTS OF INTEREST:

Boroughbridge – An ancient market town and coaching centre. Small boats abound on the river. The history of the locality is well related in a booklet available from the Information Centre near to the car park.

Aldborough – The ancient cross, 14th century St Andrew's Church, the green with its maypole, and the museum, make the extension not only very pleasant but fascinating.

REFRESHMENTS:

Readily obtained from a large variety of establishments in Boroughbridge.

Walk 33   **WHIXLEY AND ALLERTON**   5m (8km)

Maps: OS Sheets Landranger 105; Pathfinder SE 45/55.

Fairly gentle walking, much of it on surfaced tracks and quiet roads, as well as field paths.

Start: The Bay Horse Hotel in Stonegate, Whixley.

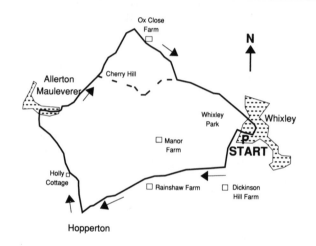

Walk westward to the Knaresborough Road and turn left along it. Pass a minor farm road on the right and walk uphill. Near to the top, and a field's length from Dickinson Hill Farm, turn right through a gate and walk along the side of the hedge through two fields. Reach an open field and cross over to the left of the hedge corner opposite. Continue ahead to the field corner and turn left to a gap in the hedge near a telegraph pole. Pass through and cross straight over the field to a stile. Bear slightly to the left of a pond and go over a small hill to reach a fence. If this proves difficult to cross, a gate can be reached to the right, otherwise cross and walk towards the corner between a line of trees and the A59. Cross the stile here, and cross the road. Turn right to the nearby layby.

Near to the end of the layby, cross the fence at a gap in the hedge, walk over the small field and negotiate the ditch at a narrow point slightly to the right. Hopefully a plank bridge may be installed, but crossing is usually not difficult. Turn left to a stile, cross and turn right along the fence side. Go left in the field corner to a large gap in the hedge. Pass through and walk to the left of the buildings of High Farm, aiming to the left of a low stone wall in the field corner. Cross over the fence to a road. Turn right and walk past the Mason Arms Inn to the A59. Follow the footpath left and across the road, past the front of Holly Cottage, and turn right along the Allerton road. Follow this up to St Martin's Church at Allerton Mauleverer. The entrance to **Allerton Park** is opposite.

Follow the road, now a bridleway, right (north) of the church and past buildings. It bears left to reach a T-junction. The track to the right here gives an alternative way back to Whixley if you wish. Otherwise walk ahead along the side of the plantation. Reach a corner and bear right along a wide track through the narrow plantation. On emerging, continue ahead and bear left along the right-hand side of the hedge to reach an open field. Bear half right towards the end of the hedge by a holly bush, pass through the gap and walk along the track past Ox Close Farm. The track, still a bridleway, becomes a tarmacked farm road which leads past junctions with minor tracks to **Whixley**.

After entering the village, divert left to the Church of the Ascension, along the short lane, signposted 'Footpath'. Return and continue along Church Street. Turn right at the end to Stonegate and the start.

POINTS OF INTEREST:

Allerton Park – Has extensive grounds, including a caravan site, well hidden, and an unusual house. Antique cars and musical machines are displayed. Open to the public on Sundays, 1–5pm.

Whixley – Is a long established village, generally well maintained and with a high proportion of large houses with beautiful grounds. The old church retains a Norman window and font.

Walk 34 **HOVINGHAM** 5m (8km)

Maps: OS Sheets Landranger 100; Pathfinder SE 67/77.

An easy walk through parkland and deciduous woods.

Start: At 656753, a wide grassy area one mile west of Hovingham.

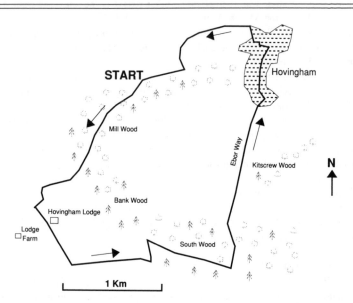

Leave the road and walk along the waymarked grassy track, keeping the stream on your left, into the wooded area. Pass through the gate and into the field still keeping the stream on your left.

Turn left on reaching the stoned road and follow it past Hovingham Lodge. Go down a hill and then up the other side to where the road turns sharply right. Here take the path that goes through the gate to the left of the hedge. Continue through two further gates until you reach the Sheriff Hutton road.

Turn left up the hill. At the top turn right into the forest and follow the path that bends round to the left. Keep on this track to a junction where the path goes right and left. Turn left and continue, admiring the view, into Hovingham.

Pass slowly through the village, passing **Hovingham Hall**. Cross the stream near the garage, then turn left. When the road turns right follow the stream past the farmyard (or go through the farmyard) then follow the farm track. Turn left and cross the strangely ornate bridge before carrying on to rejoin the Hovingham to Coulton road. Turn right to return to the start point.

POINTS OF INTEREST:
Hovingham Hall – Home of the Worsley family and childhood home of the Duchess of Kent. Good views over Ryedale.

REFRESHMENTS:
The Malt Shovel, Hovingham (tel no: 065 382 264).

Walk 35　　　　　**TERRINGTON**　　　　　5m (8km)

Maps: OS Sheets Landranger 100; Pathfinder SE 67/77.
An easy walk through agricultural land.
Start: At 673707, Terrington Church.

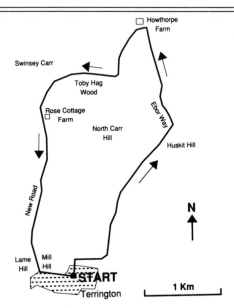

Leave the road heading north on a green lane and go on past the chapel on your left. The track leads into Terrington Hall School playing fields. Turn right, keeping the wall to your right. Continue on and through a gap in the hedge to reach an arable field.

Follow the hedge, keeping it on your right. Turn left on reaching the next field and continue with the hedge on your left for about ³/₄ mile. Pass over a plank bridge and scramble up the small hill beyond through the bushes. Keep the hedge on your left until you reach a farm track.

Turn left and continue along this track, towards Howthorpe Farm. After passing through the gateway turn left between the hedge and the pond into a grass field. Carry on, keeping the hedge on your left, then go through a gate towards the corner. Keep straight on with the large hedge and a stream on your right.

Soon you will see a gate and a bridge over the stream. Cross over and continue up the hill with the hedge on your left. Go through a gate into a grass field, following a track bearing to the right towards the right of the farm buildings. Pass through the farmyard to the right of the house. The walking is easy now. Soon you will reach a tarmac road, passing a picturesque lake on your right, once part of Wiganthorpe Estate. It is a short walk now back to Terrington and the start of the walk.

POINTS OF INTEREST:
Picturesque landscaping around Wiganthorpe Park.

REFRESHMENTS:
The Bay Horse, Terrington, Coneysthorpe (tel no: 065 384 255).

Maps: OS Sheets Landranger 100; Pathfinder SE 67/77.

A very easy walk through farmland and ancient deciduous woodland.

Start: At 704732 on the Slingsby to Castle Howard Road.

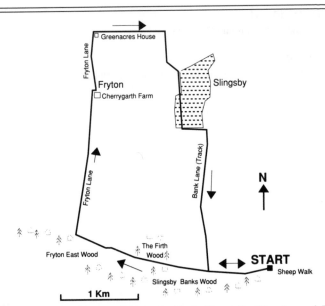

Park at the top of the 'Sheepwalk' is on the Castle Howard to Slingsby road. From here there are vast views over Ryedale. The ground under the trees is a mass of flowers, especially in May.

Start by walking west along the track which follows the ridge. Looking south you have excellent views of Castle Howard, while to the north there are views of Ryedale and the North York Moors.

Continue on the track for about a mile until you reach the road from Fryton to Baxton Howe. Turn right, cross the Hovingham to Malton road and go through the little hamlet of Fryton before turning right on to the old railway track from Helmsley to Malton immediately after the renovated railway cottage.

Continue until you reach a stile on the right. Go over into Slingsby Allotments.

After leaving the field follow the stoned road into Slingsby, past the playing fields and the ruined castle. You may wish to visit the village green where a maypole still stands.

When you reach the Malton to Hovingham road, cross over and follow the road to **Castle Howard**. Where the road bends to the left, the path continues straight on along a farm track until it peters out in an arable field at the top of the hill.

Turn right and then left by the hedge. The path soon joins the outward path. Turn left and again enjoy the views to north and south before returning to the start.

POINTS OF INTEREST:

Castle Howard – Better known to TV addicts as *Brideshead* this beautiful castle is open to the public. A stately home set in beautiful surroundings. Within the house is a Costumes Gallery containing period costumes. There is a nature walk through Ray Wood. It is open daily from 25 March until 31 October, 11am – 4.30pm. A plant centre, rose gardens, the grounds and cafeteria are open from 10am (tel no: 065 384 333).

REFRESHMENTS:
The Grapes Inn, Slingsby, Hovingham (tel no: 065 382 229).

Walk 37 **THIRSK** 5m (8km)

Maps: OS Sheets Landranger 99; Pathfinder SE 38/48.

An easy walk, no climbing, riverside wildlife.

Start: In Thirsk Market Place, but beware – Monday market days can be crowded.

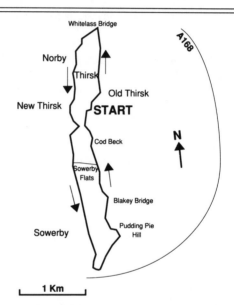

Follow Millgate out of the Market Place and through St James's Green to join the A61. Turn left along the path on the very wide left-hand grass verge until the last of the houses is passed. Cross Whitelass Beck on the road bridge and continue for a further 150 yards to a wide field gate on your left. Go through it. A footpath leads you across a field to Cod Beck. Turn left and follow a path through some genuine meadows into a small wood. Passing through this wood you reach a footbridge opposite the County Council Highways Depot. Cross and follow the beckside path to St Mary's parish church. Follow Kirkgate back into the market place, passing Thirsk Hall on your right, and a little further on the same side is the famous vet's surgery. Almost opposite this is the interesting local museum.

Now leave **Thirsk** market place by turning right towards Sowerby. Just after passing the Catholic church take the footpath leading straight ahead to Sowerby Flats (not a multi-floor block, Flats is a name for old flood plains). At the end of this surfaced footpath a path goes in a diagonal line across pasture to Cod Beck. This is a useful path if you want to shorten the walk. Continue along the footpath through Sowerby until you reach the southern end of the village. Just before you reach the A19 overpass you will see a pack horse bridge on your right built in about 1672. On your left is a signed path taking you to the ancient tumulus called Pudding Pie Hill. Turn left here to join Blakey Lane. Turn left and cross Cod Beck on the bridge.

On your right-hand side across Blakey Lane Bridge is a stile which is the start of a beckside footpath back to Sowerby Flats. Both this section of Cod Beck and that encountered earlier in the day, hold reasonable sized trout, with this section also having some big pike. Anywhere you are liable to see a heron, the flash of a kingfisher, or even a sinister mink! Although this watercourse is called a beck it is, in fact, a small river which drains a major part of the western side of the North York Moors. It is shown on old maps as the River Codbeck, joining the River Swale about 3 miles further downstream.

The best route back to the Thirsk market place from Sowerby Flats is the footpath behind the hospital and swimming baths joining the market place at the Three Tuns Hotel – the original Manor House – where the nationally known local weather prophet, Bill Foggit can be found some lunch times!

POINTS OF INTEREST:
Thirsk – Well known as a horse racing town, and lesser known as the home of James Herriot the vet. St Mary's Church is claimed to be the most spectacular perpendicular church in North Yorkshire. It was built from 1430. Thirsk Hall was built in 1720. Thirsk Folk Museum is open from Easter to the end of September 1000hrs–1700hrs. (tel no: 0845 22755). The town also has a bird museum.

REFRESHMENTS:
There are many inns, hotels, cafes and restaurants in the town and some good food and ale is available.

Walk 38   **BARTON** $5^1/_2$m (9km)

Maps: OS Sheets Landranger 93; Pathfinder NZ 20/30 & 21/31.
An easy walk along pleasant country lanes and green tracks.
Start: The Half Moon Inn, Barton.

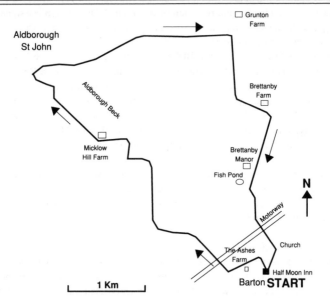

From the Half Moon Inn cross the road to a public footpath sign and continue to the top of a carriage drive. There, go through a bridle gate and turn left past some farm buildings along a cart-track. Stay on this track, crossing the motorway, to reach the B6275, Piercebridge to Scotch Corner road, after 1 mile. Turn right along the road, using the verge where necessary, for $^1/_2$ mile. Just beyond a junction with a lane on your right, turn left along a cart-track to Micklow Farm. At the farmhouse turn left, briefly, then right, round two farm cottages. Continue through a field gate and along another cart-track all the way to reach a lane at Aldbrough St John. Turn right along the lane crossing Aldborough Beck and going half-right to join a narrow lane coming from the village green on your left. Turn right along this lane until the B6275 is reached.

    Go directly across and through a facing field gate. Keep straight ahead close to a hedge on the right, across two fields. Now keep alongside a hedge on the left until a farm road is reached. Turn right along it in the direction of the Brettanby Estate. The right of way is between Brettanby Farm buildings and some sheds, then right along a tarmac farm road past Brettanby Manor, a fine old Victorian country manor, home of the Vaux family for 80 years. As soon as Barton Beck is crossed turn left, leaving the tarmac road. Cross a stile and continue downstream for a few yards to go through a field gate. Walk round two sides of the field ahead to reach Brettanby Lane. Turn left along this lane for $^1/_2$ mile, re-crossing the motorway, and passing Barton church to reach the Half Moon Inn, the start of the walk.

POINTS OF INTEREST:
The fishponds seen upstream of the bridge over Barton Beck once supplied water to a waterwheel in a nearby building.

REFRESHMENTS:
The Stanwick Arms, Aldbrough St John (tel no: 0325 374258).

Walk 39   BILSDALE WEST MOOR   6m (10km)

Maps: OS Sheets Landranger 100; Outdoor Leisure 26.

A moderate walk over moor and arable land. Over 800 feet of climbing, in one long slog!

Start: The Sun Inn on the B1257 Stokesley road eight miles north of Helmsley.

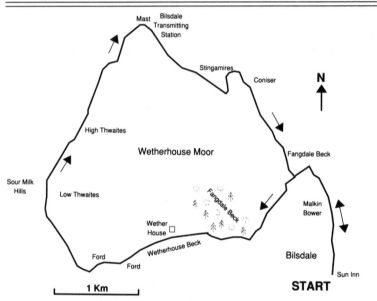

It is best to ask permission at the Sun Inn if parking there. Follow the road north for about $^1/_2$ mile. After passing the church on your right turn left into the village of Fangdale Beck (the telephone box at this junction is one of the few in Britain to be painted green), crossing the River Seph.

Once in the village the road forks. Take the left-hand fork and follow it until it becomes a farm track leading to Malkin Bower. About 200 yards before the farm turn right through a gate and follow the footpath uphill through fields to the corner of a wood. Go through a gate and continue uphill on the farm track until you exit on to the moor at another gate.

Turn left here and walk a few yards to reach an indistinct footpath that leads uphill to your right across the moor. Follow this path for a good $^1/_4$ mile to the brow of the hill. You should see a line of shooting butts to your left.

To your right is the remains of a small farm called Wether House, reputedly a drovers inn called the Wider Tree on a junction of several old roads. It was called Wider House in the 1841 census.

Follow the indistinct footpath down the declevity of Wetherhouse Beck until you reach the ford below Sike House (another ruin). About 300 yards further on the path joins a bridle path. Turn right here and follow the path to reach an old moorland track south of Low Thwaites. Take this northwards passing High Thwaite. Both Low and High Thwaite are further ruined farms. It is interesting to note that in the 1851 census these two farms were home to twenty one people, including children.

Pass a moorland pond on your left and continue northwards for about $^1/_4$ mile until the moorland track forks. Take the fork going straight ahead towards the Bilsdale transmission mast. When you reach the mast turn right and leave the high moor by the service road. This is not a public right of way, the actual right of way snakes about the hillside, but in practice nobody seems to object to walkers using it to reach Stingamires Farm.

At Stingamires turn right and follow a farm path to Coniser Farm. Continue through the farm and across a few fields to Stone House Farm. Here the path becomes a little obscure. Go right past the buildings and leave the farm track by a gate in front of you at a left-hand bend. The path continues across three fields back to Fangdale Beck, from where you return to the **Sun Inn** and the **Thatched Cruck House** at Spout House.

POINTS OF INTEREST:

The Sun Inn – Typical local of years ago, no food, spartan, run by the same family for hundreds of years (who also farm the area) but the landlord is a wealth of local information providing you can understand good Cleveland dialect.

The Thatched Cruck House – (the original inn) at Spout House, purchased by the National Park Authority, open to the public, check with the National Park Information Service:– Danby Moors Centre 0287 60540, Sutton Bank Information Centre 0845 597426.

Walk 40   SUTTON BANK   6$\frac{1}{2}$m (10km)

Maps: OS Sheets Landranger 100; Outdoor Leisure 26.

A walk in old woodland and nature reserves.

Start: The National Trust car park on Sutton Bank.

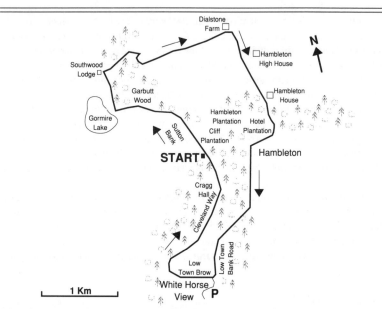

Walk from the car park to the brow of the hill. On the right-hand side of the road you will see a signpost marked 'Cleveland Way'. Follow this towards the top of Whitestone Cliff. Within a few yards you will see a sign for the start of the Sutton Bank Nature Trail (leaflets available in the **Information Office**). Follow the track for about 300 yards to a point where the Nature Trail goes downhill. The Cleveland Way continues for a further hundred miles to Filey! The downhill track towards Gormire Lake is steep in places through Garbutt Wood Nature Reserve. Several paths lead off the main route but continue on the Nature Trail to Marker No 10. Now leave the Trail and go downhill to the edge of the lake. Local folklore claims that Gormire is bottomless, but it is in fact quite shallow.

Turn right and follow the lakeside path. This soon starts to climb: follow it for almost $\frac{1}{2}$ mile, the latter part on a timber walkway over bogland. At the end of the walkway a bridlepath signposted for Thirlby Bank climbs up right. Continue uphill for almost $^1/_2$ mile to rejoin the Cleveland Way. Turn right for 200yds to a small gate on your left. A few yards further on is a stile, also left. Go over this and keep the field edge on your right to reach a signpost for Dialstone House. Follow this until the farm is reached. Turn right and follow the minor road for 100 yards to a T-junction. Straight ahead of you at this junction is a bridlepath that leads in front of Hambleton High House, and across the racehorse training gallops to reach Hambleton House. Follow its driveway out to the A170 at the Hambleton Inn.

Turn right and follow the main road for 100 yards to the minor road to White Horse Bank on your left. Follow the road for a mile or, better, use a forest track on the right-hand side. Continue past the Yorkshire Gliding Club buildings on your right to reach the public car park on your left. Almost opposite this a track leads you across 150 yards of moor to the **White Horse**.

The path continues for a little over a mile back to the start. WARNING – there is a very high crag on the left in places: do not let children out of your sight.

Just below you on the left is Hood Hill, where Cistercian Monks settled when they moved from Furness to Yorkshire, prior to going to Old Byland in 1143 and later still to Byland Abbey in 1177. On the southern end of Hood Hill are the very slight remains of a Halifax bomber.

POINTS OF INTEREST:

National Park Information Office – Open daily in summer, Sundays only in winter. (tel no: 0845 597426).

The White Horse – The White Horse of Kilburn is one of Yorkshire's most famous landmarks, visible from 30 miles or more away. The Horse is a fine viewpoint with York Minster visible if you know where to look! A coin-in-the-slot telescope is available near the tail of the Horse.

REFRESHMENTS:

The Hambleton Inn, (tel no: 0845 597202).
The Yorkshire Gliding Club, (tel no: 0845 597237).

Walk 41   OSMOTHERLEY   6$\frac{1}{2}$m (10km)

Maps: OS Sheets Landranger 93, 99 & 100; Outdoor Leisure 26.
Easy walking in fields, woodland and marginal moorland.
Start: Osmotherley.

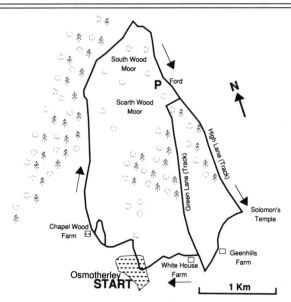

Take the road that leaves the village, northwards and uphill. About $\frac{1}{2}$ mile after the last of the houses you come to Ruebury Lane, a track on your left-hand side. Follow this for 300 yards to where the track forks near a direction pillar pointing out all the long distance views across the Vale of Mowbray. Take the right-hand fork if you wish to visit the **Lady Chapel**. The footpath back to your route from the chapel is not a public right of way but its use has not been objected to.

If you are not going to the chapel, continue straight on, following part of the Cleveland Way until you reach the forest above **Mount Grace Priory**. The detour back from Lady Chapel joins your route just above Chapel Wood Farm.

Once through the forest gate, bear right and leave the main forest track. Follow the track uphill for $\frac{1}{4}$ mile, crossing the ancient earthworks and some old, riven oak fence. Continue, keeping the moor wall on your right-hand side, for $\frac{1}{4}$ mile until you reach the British Telecom station on Scarth Wood Moor. Continue in the same direction, going through a small gate until the track goes through the gate in the right-hand wall. Beyond the track splits. Take the left-hand one, going downhill to join the road at Scarth Nick.

Turn right and follow the road until you come to the watersplash at Sheepwash. Now follow the unsurfaced county road (the ancient Drovers Road) uphill ahead to reach the forest corner.

If the weather has been wet, the forest section can be muddy, and you can take a drier route as follows. Continue on the Drove Road for almost a mile until you join the Snilesworth road near Solomon's Temple. Turn right and follow the road until you reach Rose Cottage – a rebuilt house, just after a cattle grid. Just beyond turn off the road to the right following the track to White House Farm.

If there is little risk of mud, or if you don't mind it, turn right at the forest corner. Half way – about 150 yards – towards the reservoir (which has a picnic area) a stile takes you into the forest. A straight well-defined path leads you right through the forest, and continues through fields until you drop down to the White House farm track.

Follow the signed footpath past the farm, keeping the buildings on your left, and drop down to the footbridge over Cod Beck. A steep climb up through the trees brings you into a field at the back of **Osmotherley**, a narrow path between gardens takes you into Back Lane, and a further path between houses takes you back into the village.

POINTS OF INTEREST:
Lady Chapel – A medieval hermitage chapel. Once the site of Catholic pilgrimages.
Mount Grace Priory – Fine remains of a Carthusian priory. A National Trust site reached from the A19.
Osmotherley – Famous for its associations with John Wesley who preached here many times.

REFRESHMENTS:
The Queen Catherine Hotel, (tel no: 0609 83209).
The Golden Lion, (tel no: 0609 83526).
The Kings Head, (mile away) (tel no: 0609 83207).

Walk 42   **INGLEBY GREENHOW**   7m (11km)

Maps: OS Sheets Landranger 93 & 94; Outdoor Leisure 26.
This walk offers some of the finest walking in the Cleveland Hills.
Start: Ingleby Greenhow.

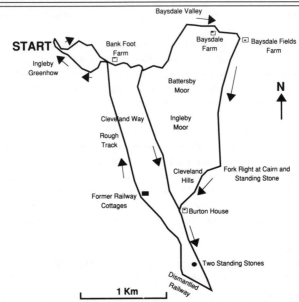

Leave Ingleby Greenhow along the Battersby road and after $^1/_4$ mile turn right along the
road for 1 mile to Bank Foot Farm. Just past the farm go left through a facing gate and
go along the rough signposted road through Battersby Plantation, climbing steeply up
Ingleby Bank. We now follow the route of an old coach road, winding first right, then
left, then right again. At the top of the 500ft climb the views are superb, panoramas of
the Cleveland Plain, including Roseberry Topping and Captain Cook's Monument. For
a shorter walk turn sharp right, keeping to the coach road, and climb on to Ingleby
Moor, joining the Cleveland Way. Follow this southwards for $1^1/_2$ miles to Burton
Howe to rejoin the longer walk.

For a longer walk leave the coach road at the sharp bend and follow the cairned
moorland path on the left which curves to the left to join the Cleveland Way. Turn left
along the Way for $^1/_2$ mile to reach a road through two gates. Here leave the Cleveland

Way, passing Baysdale Farm on the right. Cross Black Beck on a medieval bridge, where a misleading notice incorrectly says 'Private Road'. The farm road ahead is a right of way. As you approach **Baysdale Fields Farm** turn right through a white painted gate to cross some fields aiming for a rusty gate beside a broken stile below a plantation. Go through the gate and along a rising forest track and out on to Ingleby Moor through a white gate. Go southwards along a clear track and after $1^1/_2$ miles look for a standing stone and a cairn on your right. The way is now right, (south-west) over cairned moor along Middle Head Top. Fork left along a moorland track to reach, in just under 1 mile, the cairned Bronze Age burial site of **Burton Howe**.

Continue, to join the Cleveland Way, and turn left along it for some glorious walking, southwards, past some grouse butts and, on your right, two standing stones, to reach Bloworth Crossing. Now turn right along the dismantled railway, sharing the next $1/_4$ mile with the Cleveland Way, the Coast to Coast route and the Lyke Wake Walk. Where these walks swing left up to Botton Head, stay on the railway for 1 mile to reach Ingleby Incline. The way is now down it on an average gradient of 1:5 to reach the Forestry Commission road. Follow this for 2 miles back to Bank Foot from where you go left along a waymarked field path to Ingleby Greenhow and the start.

POINTS OF INTEREST:
The popular viewpoint at the top of Ingleby Bank is known locally as Turkey Nab (not shown on OS maps).
Baysdale Fields Farm – The farm stands on the site of the 12th century Cistercian nunnery shown on OS maps as Baysdale Priory and of which nothing remains.
The shorter and older of the two standing stones near Bloworth Crossing is called Jenny Bradley and the taller one has inscribed on it 'Sir W. Fowles 1838'.
Burton Howe – One of the most spectacular Bronze Age sites on the Moor. The largest round barrow is 50 foot in diameter and 89 foot high.

REFRESHMENTS
The Dudley Arms (tel no: 0642 722526).

Walk 43   GREAT AYTON   7m (11km)

Maps: OS Sheets Landranger 93; Outdoor Leisure 26.

Moderate walking across fields and along forest and moorland paths.

Start: Great Ayton.

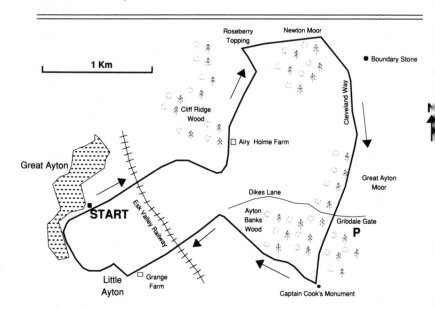

Leave Great Ayton eastwards along the High Street. Turn left along Newton Road for 80 yards then go right through a kissing gate and along a fenced path through Hall Fields, through several kissing gates and passing Cleveland Lodge on the left. Cross the Esk Valley Railway to a farm track marked 'Private Road'. Bear left to cross a stile near a gate. Follow a path with a fence to the left, climbing into Cliff Ridge Wood. There turn right along a path near the wood's edge, cross a waymarked stile and follow yellow arrows into Airy Holme Lane. Turn left to **Airy Holme Farm**, turn left in front of the farmhouse, then right, through a gate with a footpath sign. Take the bridleway ahead, which begins as a rutted track and eventually becomes a green track, for $^1/_2$ mile. Where it bifurcates, keep on the upper path, go through a handgate, and climb to the trig point on **Roseberry Topping**. Go ahead and through a second gate to rejoin the other route opposite a National Trust sign. From the sign climb east along a rutted track with a wall on the right. The route levels, then climbs again along an erosion control new path to enter Newton Moor through a gate. Turn right (south) along a path marked 'Cleveland Way', close to a wall on the right, edging Slacks Wood, passing a National Trust signpost and two boundary stones. At this point you cross from Cleveland into North Yorkshire. After a mile the path descends steeply to Gribdale Gate car park. Turn right along the road and when close to a cattle grid turn left through a gate signposted 'Cleveland Way' and climb a broad track through Ayton Banks Wood to **Captain Cook's Monument** on Easby Moor. From the monument go half-right along a moorland track, going through two isolated gateposts in the wall near the escarpment edge. Continue along the path close to a low ruined wall on your left and fork left, downhill, into a plantation. Cross a forest road and re-enter the plantation going downhill and out of the wood through a gate into a field. Keep close to the wall on your right, and at its corner turn right, downhill, along a rutted track, keeping a look out for a small gate giving access to a small wood. The path, known locally as Larmers Lane, soon becomes a lane. Continue as far as the 'Firbrook' sign. There, turn left along an unsurfaced farm road over the Esk Valley Railway and into Little Ayton. Turn right along Little Ayton Lane, passing Grange Farm. Between Holme Field and Earlham Farms turn left down an enclosed path to cross the River Leven by footbridge. The way is now diagonally half-right across a field, through a gap in its corner and half-right again over the next field. Cross a stile near a gate and take the path near the hedge on the right and cross a short fence. Continue along the Leven, beside sportsfields, and cross the footbridge over the river back into Great Ayton.

POINTS OF INTEREST:

Airy Holme Farm – James Cook came to live at the farm when he was 8 years old, his father being a local bailiff.

Roseberry Topping – Now owned by the National Trust, is Cleveland's most popular summit. The views from it across Cleveland into Durham and out to the North Sea are extensive.

Captain Cook's Monument – A sandstone obelisk, 51ft high, erected in 1827 in the memory of Captain James Cook F.R.S. the celebrated circumnavigator.

REFRESHMENTS:

There are pubs and cafés in Great Ayton.

Walk 44   OSMOTHERLY/BEACON HILL   7m (11km)

Maps: OS Sheets Landranger 93, 99 & 100; Outdoor Leisure 26.
An easy to moderate scenic walk with a couple of steep climbs.
Start: Osmotherly.

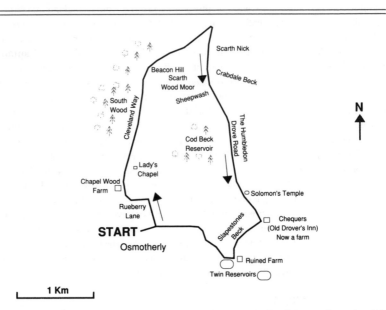

Leave Osmotherly (*see* Walk 41) along North End on the Swainby road, turning left into Ruebury Lane, signposted 'Cleveland Way'. Follow this unsurfaced lane around Ruebury Hill. Where, the lane bifurcates, at a Viewpoint Indicator, a short detour along the upper track will bring you to Lady Chapel (*see* Walk 41). The main route, along the lower track, passes Chapel Wood Farm on the left and continues through a signposted kissing gate to follow a farm track through gated fields into South Wood. Turn right at a 'Cleveland Way' signpost, climb a steep forest drive and at the top continue along the escarpment edge past a British Telecom Microwave Radio Station. Soon a white trig point is seen over a wall on your right. It marks the summit of Beacon Hill, at 982ft above sea level, the highest point on the walk. Continue with the wall on your right through a gate, across a corner stile and half-right over Scarth Wood Moor. Go down some steps to a road at Scarth Nick. Turn right along the road to The Sheepwash, the starting point for the Lyke Wake Walk, and the Shepherds Round. Cross Crabdale Beck, either fording or using the footbridge, and take the broad, uphill track along High Lane, part of the Hambleton Drive Road, which runs south from Scarth Nick to 15 miles distant Sutton Bank. After $1^1/_2$ miles the Hawnby Road is reached. Go left along it for almost $^1/_2$ mile to Slapestones where, on the left, at **Chequers**, a former ruin is now a working farm. Tea and scones can be purchased, the farm making a good butty stop.

Just beyond the farm cross Slapestones Beck and turn right at the public footpath sign. Follow the track with a wall on your left and, where it bends left, continue ahead, downhill. Cross rough pasture and go through a gate on to a green track into hidden Oakdale Valley with its twin reservoirs. Continue through another gate past derelict Oakdale House on your left and bear right to join the broad track the Cleveland Way below. Turn right along it. Cross a stile beside a gate, pass the lower reservoir and take the broad track uphill out of the wooded valley and across fields to the Hawnby Road. Turn left along it for 50 yards then right along Green Lane, and, beyond the entrance to White House Farm, turn left over a stile signposted 'Cleveland Way'. Go along the farm road, passing White House Farm on your left, and head for a telegraph pole showing a white arrow and 'Footpath' in bold letters. Cross a stile and continue downhill to bridge lovely Cod Beck, known locally as Happy Valley. Climb steeply out of the valley on railed steps and go ahead over stiled fields and an enclosed path into Back Lane. Turn right beside Bramblewick and St Anne's Cottage along a cobbled path which will bring you through Chapel Passage back into Osmotherly.

POINTS OF INTEREST:
Much of the walk coincides with the Cleveland Way and follows in the steps of the drovers.
Chequers – The restored iron sign here proclaims: '*Be not in haste. Step in and taste Ale tomorrow for nothing*'.

REFRESHMENTS:
The Three Tuns, Osmotherly (tel no: 060983 301).
The Queen Catherine, Osmotherly (tel no: 060983 209).
The Golden Lion, Osmotherly (tel no: 060983 526).

Walk 45   **HAWNBY**   7m (11km)

Maps: OS Sheets Landranger 100; Outdoor Leisure 26.

Easy. Hawnby is a delightful village, perched on a hillside and surrounded by tabular hills.

Start: At 543895 in Hawnby village.

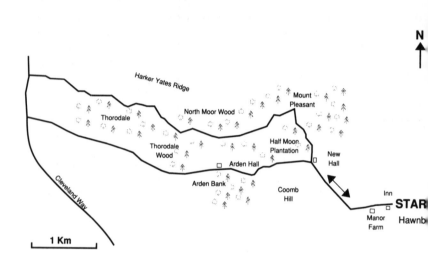

Take the Kepwick road out of Hawnby. The road is suitable for cars in its early stages, but most will use the limited parking in the village, which adds 2 miles to the walk. Whether walking or driving, make time to see lovely Hawnby Church; in springtime, the churchyard overflows with wild daffodils. From New Hall (the alternative parking spot) take the cart track between buildings on the right, going downhill between bushes. At the bottom cross a sleeper bridge over the stream and continue forward with the woodland on your left. Emerging from the woods, keep to the right side of the field until a farm track is reached. Turn left, pass through the farmyard and then left on to a farm road. Go over a cattlegrid. The gate next to it says 'Beware of the Bull' (this is Mount Pleasant Farm!). Go forward 200 yards to a triangular clump of trees. Go through the first gate on the right. This is Thorodale. Keep straight forward over fields. Arden Hall, seat of the Earls of Mexborough, can be seen to the left: part of an ancient nunnery. At a crossroads of tracks, the one to the left dipping down to a ford, go straight ahead on the track into the woods where 'Private' notices keep you on the right path.

In the wood, you may catch a glimpse of the lake down to the left. At the end of the wood, go through a gate into a secluded, open valley. Go down to the stream and follow a faint path on the right. Go up to an isolated hawthorn tree, crossing the stream as necessary. Make your way up the steep zigzag path and pause at the top to take in the view. Go up to the wall and, keeping it on your left, proceed westerly to a gate. Go through, pass some old workings and the ruins of Limekiln House, once a Drovers' Inn. The view from here is superb. Turn left on the Drove Road and go for less than $^1/_2$ mile to the cross track where the road comes up from Kepwick. Here turn left on the track which leads back to Hawnby. It goes first through open fields then, after a gate, across fields. Here the lake can be seen to the best advantage. The road slopes steeply down the side of the valley, and goes through extensive woods to Arden Hall. From here it is a mile to New Hall.

REFRESHMENTS:
The Hawnby Hotel, (tel no: 04396 202). Lunchtime bar snacks, local produce used.

Walk 46　　　**SHERIFF HUTTON**　　　7m (11km)

Maps: OS Sheets Landranger 100; Pathfinder SE 66/76.

A pleasant walk on the edge of the Howardian Hills using field tracks and paths. Parts a little muddy in wet conditions.

Start: The Main Street, Sheriff Hutton.

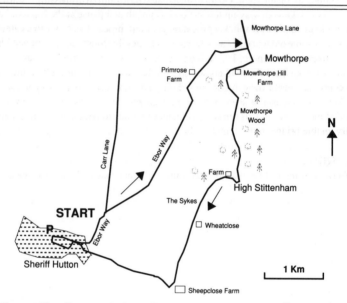

Walk past The Green and along Church End. Go through a gateway, pass farm buildings and go through a second gateway. Turn left along a footpath that follows the field boundary by the side of the hedge to a stile to a road. Turn right along the road and then left down a wide track. Soon bear right across a stile by a gate and follow the hedge and, soon, a stream. Cross a bridge and a training gallops course keeping close to the hedge to reach a wide track which crosses open fields. When a wide track is reached, turn left and follow it through open fields, across two streams and along a hedge. Pass through a gateway, turn left and walk round the field to a gap on the left. Bear right between the disused buildings of Primrose Farm and follow the good track up through gates to a road.

　　Turn right and, soon, right again along a drive to pass Mowthorpe Farm. Cross the stile ahead. Continue forward and pick up the track which bears left, downhill through Mowthorpe Wood. Turn right on reaching a track through a gateway. This bears slightly left, and crosses two streams and an open field to reach a small gateway entry into Stittenham Wood. At a T-junction, cross the stile ahead and walk uphill along the footpath, bearing right to cut through the trees. Waymarks help on this section. Reach a track, turn right for a few yards and then continue again uphill. At the southern edge of the wood, a track is reached at a wire fence. Turn right and walk downhill to a stile on the left. Cross and go uphill on a path trodden through overgrowth. Cross two stiles ahead and a third past the right-hand side of a barn at Hall Farm. Bear right to a track and turn right on it.

Pass the road junction and follow the track round to Carr Farm. Turn left in front of the buildings, pass a pond, and go through a gateway. Walk downhill towards the fence, but soon bear left to reach a gateway in the southern corner of the field. Walk across the open field towards the right-hand side of Wheatclose Farm ahead. Reach a not very visible bridge in the centre of the field and walk towards a fenced gap in the roadside hedge, right of the farm. Cross the road and pass through two gates to the right of the drive. Walk ahead along the field side to a gate and a stile, slightly to the left, in the next field. Just past a gateway on the right, cross a stile and bear slightly right to the corner of a fence to the right of Sheepclose Farm. Here turn right and cross the field to a gate. Cross the open field aiming towards **Sheriff Hutton** castle. Find the footbridge by a waymarked post. Cross this and a narrow ditch beyond into the field on the right. Aim now towards St Helen's Church. It may be easier to continue along the hedge side until a clear footpath to the church is reached on your right. Reach a gate in the wall and walk by the side of the church to Church End. Retrace your steps to the start.

POINTS OF INTEREST:

Sheriff Hutton – The castle ruin is a prominent landmark. It was important during the Wars of the Roses. St Helen's Church has a Norman tower and has box pews inside. There are stocks on The Green. Nearby Sheriff Hutton Park gardens are open to the public Monday to Friday, 10 – 4.30pm. Two long distance walking routes pass through the village, the Centurion Way and the Ebor Way. The route follows the latter to Mowthorpe Hill.

REFRESHMENTS:

The Highwayman Inn, by the Green (tel no: 03477 328).
The Castle Inn, on the main road (tel no: 03477 335).

Walk 47   **SUTTON BANK**   7m (11km)

Maps: OS Sheets Landranger 100; Outdoor Leisure 26.

Easy to moderate with just one steep descent and a gradual climb up the escarpment.

Start: The Sutton Bank Visitor Centre.

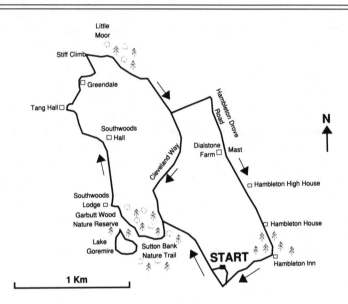

From Sutton Bank Visitor Centre cross the Cold Kirby road at the top of Sutton Bank and take the path signposted 'Cleveland Way/Nature Trail Start'. Follow the trail northwards along the escarpment's rim, passing a plantation on your right. At Nature Trail Post 3 go left, diagonally downhill, along a path into Garbutt Wood Nature Reserve. Continue through the wood, passing Post 7 and descending to Post 10. There bear right, away from Lake Gormire. Just beyond Post 13 continue straight ahead, leaving the Nature Trail, which returns to Sutton Bank. Whitestone Cliff towers 70ft over to your right. Leave **Garbutt Wood** over a stile and go west down Thirlby Bank to a lane leading to Southwoods Lodge. There take the broad, signposted, bridleway. Go through a gate marked 'Midge Holme Gate' and where tracks cross your line of walk, go ahead to where the track bends right, uphill, in the direction of Southwoods

102

Hall. There, go left on a faint path through trees, making for a gate near a dead tree trunk. Keep ahead, curving leftwards and downhill to a gate near a plantation. Go through and up a rise. At the top of turn sharp right before three hawthorn bushes. Continue parallel to a line of transmission poles. Go through a gate, then half-left to Tang Hall, turning right to pass it on your left. Turn right and take the farm road for $^1/_2$ mile to an electrified gate, using the side gate to pass it. At Greendale Farm, about $^1/_2$ mile beyond the gate, go left, uphill, through a gate waymarked with a yellow arrow, then right to another waymarked gate. Go through then left along an electrified fence. At a waymarked bridleway follow the blue arrows to a signposted junction. Go right along the 'Little Moor' route uphill through a plantation. At the top cross a stile and bear half-right across rough pasture to go between waymarked gateposts near a ruin. Continue along a bridleway between the wall and the plantation, cross a forest drive and keep straight ahead, climbing steadily, to bear right and exit through a gate on to the Cleveland Way. Turn right along it, edging the escarpment back to the Sutton Bank Visitor Centre.

Alternatively, leave the Cleveland Way after $^1/_4$ mile at a '**Hambleton Road**' signpost, go left along a bridleway to the Drove Road and turn right along it for $^1/_2$ mile, passing **Dialstone Farm** on your right. At the road junction beyond the farm cross the road and continue southwards to the A170. Turn right along it and at a sign 'White Horse Bank' take the path on your left, through Kilburn Moor Plantation to the escarpment top, where you turn right back to the start.

POINTS OF INTEREST:

Garbutt Wood – 'Donkey Stones', a soft sandstone, is mined at a small quarry near nature post 9.

Hambleton Road – Was once well used by drovers. From it there are extensive views across to Roppa Edge and into Rydale. On a clear day the twin hills of Hawnby and Eastelside are visible. Hambleton Inn is the only remaining drover's inn. It dates from the 17th century though parts have been updated since: the prices for example.

Dialstones Farm – Derives its name from the dial or weighing machine used for weighing jockeys. It was once a drover's inn.

REFRESHMENTS:

Café at Sutton Bank Visitor Centre (tel no: 0845 597426).
The Hambleton Inn, Sutton Bank (tel no: 0485 597202).

Maps: OS Sheets Landranger 100; Pathfinder SE 47/57.
*A moderately difficult walk through the undulating Howardian
Hills. Woodland, track and field paths. Fairly good underfoot.*
Start: To the west of Ampleforth in the hill top lay-by or near the
Police House.

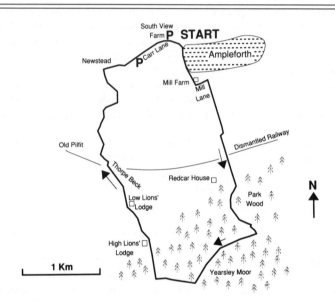

Take the clear footpath south–east between buildings and by a stream side to reach Mill
Farm and the road. Turn left and reach a stile at the bend. Go over and follow the grass
track to a footbridge. Keep by the stream side to a road. Despite the **Wildlife Reserve**
notice, cross ahead over the open space and find a narrow path into woodland between
trees. Soon you climb up a small slope on your right to gain a track by the side of the
Lower Fish Pond. Continue along the bank and then join a wider track, still maintaining
direction. This track bears left and straightens. Reach a gap on the right and pass
through by the side of the first of the two Lower Fish Ponds. Turn left along the track
to a junction. Nearby, a narrow path left goes to the second pond. At the junction, turn
right and uphill. Follow this main track past a house and through a gateway. The track

bears left and right, but just before the bearing off to the right, you turn left along a narrower grass track. Follow this well-used path, keeping straight ahead at all crossings, to reach the Yearsley road at a junction.

Cross and walk along the Thirsk road through woodland until a gate on the right gives access to an open field. Cross to reach High Lions' Lodge. Pass through the gate and bear left across a fence, past the front of the newer building and go over a second fence. A gate to the right may be easier if this is obstructed. Walk downhill with trees on your left, reach a gate and continue with a stone wall on your right. Bear a little left round woodland, go through a gate and maintain direction to another gate. Reach a fence on your left and Low Lions' Lodge. Pass through gates to the right of the farm to walk on the track past the right-hand side of the large barn. Follow the farm road ahead down to a junction. Turn left across the disused railway and right at a second junction. Follow the road and track past Old Pilfit. The track bends right round woodland. Turn left through a gate, and follow the hedge on the right. At the end of the hedge, turn left across a field to a double stile. Walk downhill to a gate with a hedge on the right.

Turn right to a fence enclosing a pond and right again uphill aiming to the left of the summit. Descend to the left of a line of bushes. Pass through the centre of three gates, and bear left across the field aiming towards the centre of three more gates. Bear left across the field, aiming towards the centre of a group of trees on a hill. Cross a stile and footbridge, and maintain direction over a fence to the right of a large tree, uphill to the top right corner of the field and, with a fence on your right, reach a road. Turn right to reach your car.

POINTS OF INTEREST:
Wildlife Reserve – Fine woodland. No permit needed for our way.

REFRESHMENTS:
Available during normal pub hours at either:
The White Swan, (tel no: 04393 239).
The White Horse, in Ampleforth (tel no: 04393 378).

Walk 49   **WELBURN**   7m (11km)

Maps: OS Sheets Landranger 100; Pathfinder SE 67/77.

A moderately difficult walk through undulating countryside, with pleasant woodland and good views. One very short swampy section.

Start: In the village of Welburn.

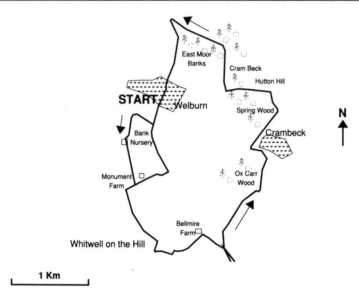

Take the road south up to the church and the track ahead. Turn right just before the line of trees. Just past a bend, turn left through a gap in the trees. Cross a stile into a field and go through a gate to the front of **Monument Farm**. Go through the gate on its right. Turn left after passing through a second gate and quickly right and left through others. Walk towards Whitwell along the field edge and turn right along the waymarked path at its end. Turn left through the second of two gates and continue on the right of the hedge. York Minster and Sheriff Hutton Castle may be seen from here. Cross stiles, passing a single tree after the second, and follow the fence left to reach a stile on the right. Use the path to the left of a house drive. Turn left at the road, and left at a junction to St John's Church, Whitwell-on-the-Hill. A path next to the church follows the field edge to the York road.

Cross, despite the barrier, and just a little left, cross a stile and bear left to follow the left of the hedge to the road by Bellmire Farm. Walk through the farm gate and bear right across the field to a gate and a track downhill to the right. Turn left along the track below. A little way uphill near a hedge, bear left to a stile and gate into woodland and follow the narrow, wet path to a wider track and a road. Take the track opposite and a less distinct path ahead where the track goes uphill. The path bears left, uphill at first, then levelling. Reach a stile, cross and continue to a road. Turn left.

Cross the main road and turn right over Crambeck Bridge. Turn left up the track to Hutton Hill Farm but turn left before the gate at the farm to enter a field. Descend to a gate, go a little left, then cross a bridge over Cram Beck. Go straight uphill using trodden paths through damp overgrowth to reach a stile. At a gate beyond, turn right at the track junction. The track narrows and enters woodland. Keep right at a junction and walk uphill to the Four Faces Monument. Soon, take the track left along the edge of the wood. Castle Howard (*see* Walk 36) is close here. A diversion through the gate brings you close to the Pyramid and a good view. At a junction by a gate, turn sharp left downhill keeping to the well-used track which bears right to reach a footbridge and a field. A clear path across this returns you to Welburn.

POINTS OF INTEREST:
Monument Farm – See nearby a monument to an Earl of Carlisle. The track to the right gives a way to Kirkham Abbey now in view.

REFRESHMENTS:
The Crown and Cushion, Welburn (tel no: 0653 81 304). Daily 12–2pm, 7–11pm, Mondays, food summer only. Sunday close 10.30pm.

Walk 50   **KEPWICK**   7m (11km)

Maps: OS Sheets Landranger 99 & 100; Outdoor Leisure 26.

Moderate walk on arable farm land and marginal moorland, 200m of climbing.

Start: The Church, Nether Silton.

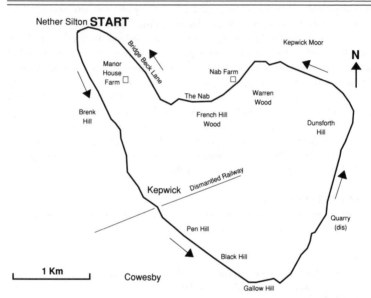

Just past the church, right, is a broad field gate. Go through. To your right you will see a large standing stone dated 1765 marking the site of the Old Manor House. In the bottom left-hand corner of this field there is a stile. Go over and continue across the next three small fields in almost a straight line crossing stiles in each fence. In the bottom left-hand corner of the last field the stile takes you over a small ditch. Turn right and head for the small wood keeping the field fence on your right. Go through the wood. Two well marked footbridges bring you into a field where you keep the fence on your left. Cross the track of the dismantled tramway to reach a field path that brings you to the road near Kepwick.

Cross this road and go through a broad field gate. To your right you will see a white broken column monument, but ignore this and go uphill, crossing a field to a gate through the drystone wall. Go through this gate and continue uphill, leftwards, on a well-used bridle path. In early summer this area is awash with rhododendrons. Continue for a mile until you are almost on the moor top at Gallow Hill. Go through the boundary wall on your left and follow the bridlepath diagonally uphill for $^1/_2$ mile.

Go through a gate to join the ancient Drovers Road at the highest point of the walk. Turn left and follow this green lane for $^1/_2$ mile, crossing the partly surfaced road from Kepwick to Hawnby. You will come to what looks like a pile of stones on your right – the remains of Limekiln House, an old Drovers' Inn. Alas, no more!

On the left, opposite the old inn, is a gate. At times this gate has a warning notice on it regarding adders – don't worry, they won't harm you if you don't harm them. Go through the gate and follow the well-marked footpath downhill and off the moor for a mile to Nab Farm.

Exit from the farm down the farm driveway to the road, turn right here and follow the minor road for a mile to **Nether Silton** and the start.

POINTS OF INTEREST:

Nether Silton – The manor house marker stone has cryptic markings, each letter depicts each word of the following:

Here The Grand Old Manor House Stood
The Black Beams Were Oak The Great Walls Were Good
The Walls At The East Wing Are Hidden Here
ATCLABWHEY
AD1765
AW, PSAYAA
Apart from the date the last three lines are unknown.

REFRESHMENTS:

The Gold Cup public house (tel no: 0609 83416). Open all usual hours, meals, b & b, run by a Swedish family.

Walk 51   KIRKHAM PRIORY   8m (13km)

Maps: OS Sheets Landranger 100; Pathfinder SE 66/76.

Fairly easy walking with a few small hills only. Quite flat along the pleasant River Derwent. Some woodland.

Start: Kirkham Priory.

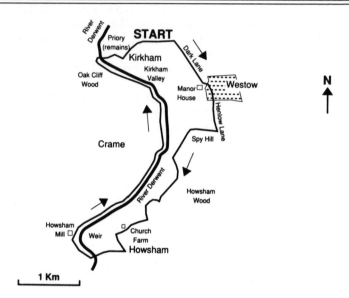

Walk easterly along the road uphill and turn left at the junction. Opposite the Firby road, a track, Dark Lane, leads to Westow, and the worst of our road walking is done. Turn left at the end of the track into Westow and then right past the Blacksmith's Arms. Continue ahead at the junction, going over a hill to a signposted gap on the right. Follow the sign along the field edge to the top of **Spy Hill**. Pass through a gate ahead and bear left downhill to gates at the opposite corner of the field. Pass through the left-hand gate on to a track into Howsham Wood. Keep left and then straight on at two junctions and arrive at a sharp right-hand bend. Do not take this, but walk ahead down what can be a muddy track. The mud is usually less deep on the left-hand side. Turn right at the bottom. Reach a stile on your left, cross and walk downhill to a footbridge and then up along the hedge.

Pass a gate to one track on the right and turn through the next. Follow this track, crossing stiles, into **Howsham**. Turn left up the road, right at the road junction and descend to Howsham Bridge. Cross and go over the stile on your right. Follow the riverside path to a footbridge and up a small slope. **Howsham Weir** is at your side here.

The footpath goes a few yards from the river to reach a gate after which it generally keeps to the riverside but is always clear. Howsham Hall – now a school – is passed on the opposite bank. Approaching Kirkham, cross a stile into a narrow stretch of woodland. The higher paths here are usually easier and you soon emerge by the weir at Kirkham, a pleasant spot with good views of the **Priory**. Cross the field to a stile and return to your car.

POINTS OF INTEREST:

Spy Hill – Well named. In clear weather many landmarks can be seen including Castle Howard and Sheriff Hutton Castle.

Howsham – A pleasant village. Note the sundial on the farm building.

Howsham Weir – A reminder that boats were once able to navigate up the Derwent to Malton. The lock area is clear. Efforts have been made to re-open the river but these have been strongly resisted by conservation groups. It is an excellent river for fishing and is popular for canoeing. The canoeists can be very entertaining near the weirs!

Kirkham Priory – A well maintained ruin. Founded in 1130AD by Augustinian monks. Open from 10am to 6pm summer, 4pm winter. Nearby is a garden centre and coffee house open up to 5.30pm. A footpath by the side of the latter which crosses the railway may prove to be worth exploring as it passes part of the way through Kirkham Gorge.

REFRESHMENTS:

The Blacksmith's Arms, Westow (tel no: 065 381 365).

Walk 52   **KILBURN**   8m (13km)

Maps: OS Sheets Landranger 100; Outdoor Leisure 26.

An undulating walk along woodland and field paths and tracks linking Kilburn and the Byland abbey. A little muddy in places.

Start: By the church and inn, Low Kilburn.

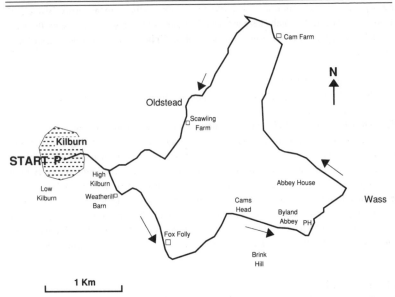

Walk through the churchyard and along the path uphill, through gates, to reach a road. Turn left past the village green in High Kilburn. At a bend, take the track on the right, through a gate and past Weatherill Barn. Turn left after a kissing gate, and cross a field to a stile. Follow the enclosed path to a quiet road. Turn right and pass Fox Folly Farm. Shortly, turn left at a bend and go over a stile by the side of a double gate. Walk with the fence on the right past a footpath junction and through a gate. The footpath provides a possible extension to **Coxwold**. Reach a small stream and cross by stepping stones. Turn left through the trees to an open field and a footpath junction near Cam Head Farm. Turn right with the hedge on your left. Change to the left of the hedge at the field corner but maintain your direction. Cross two stiles and an open field, heading towards a large tree. Walk along the higher part of the next field, parallel to the fence, to reach the road at **Byland Abbey**. Turn left round the side of the abbey to reach a stone walled bridge on the left.

Walk up the drive to Abbey House and turn right, through a gate just before the buildings. After a second gate, bear left, uphill, towards the right of a group of large trees. Cross the stile and bear left through gates to reach a track. Wass is reached to the right, but we turn left, uphill, through woodland. A stile is found ahead of you at a track junction. Cross and continue uphill soon bearing right, not descending, to find an indistinct track bearing left to a stile. Bear left along a forest track which descends before rising above a deepening valley on the right. Part can be muddy. Ignore side tracks. The main track levels and bears right to reach the edge of the wood. Go through the gate ahead and follow the wide, field-side, track to Cam Farm. Walk along the side of the barns. Pass through two gateways by the side of the farm and bear left, in front of a nicely restored building, along a track to a gate.

Use the main track ahead, ignoring others, as it goes downhill and round a sharp left bend. It soon turns right and, eventually, right again to reach the road at Oldstead. Turn left towards the village to reach Scawling Farm. Pass through the gate, through a second gate and turn left along a track. Cross the stile at the next gate and continue ahead along the field side to another stile. Bear right, downhill, towards the end of a line of bushes, and then left to a bridge over a small stream. Ascend through a small gap in the hedge and turn right along a footpath. This soon bears left and reaches a fence. Find the gate at the side and follow the enclosed path to reach a road. Turn left and follow the road back to High Kilburn. A footpath alternative on the right is a little harder. Retrace your steps to **Low Kilburn**.

POINTS OF INTEREST:

Byland Abbey – Now a ruin. It was built by monks who moved here from Old Byland because it was too close to Rievaulx Abbey.

Coxwold – A fine village nearby, one of the prettiest in Yorkshire, well worth a visit.

Low Kilburn – Famous for Thompson's mouse-marked furniture. The White Horse is to the North.

REFRESHMENTS:

The Forresters' Arms, Kilburn (tel no: 03476 386).
The Abbey Inn, Byland (tel no. 03476 204).
The Black Swan Inn, Oldstead (tel no: 03476 387).

Walk 53   **CASTLE HOWARD**   8m (13km)

Maps: OS Sheets Landranger 100; Pathfinder SE 67/77 & 66/76.
A fairly gentle walk taking in the grounds of Castle Howard and a wooded ridge with pleasant views.
Start: Cars can be parked at the side of the road through Castle Howard at the northern end of the Great Lake.

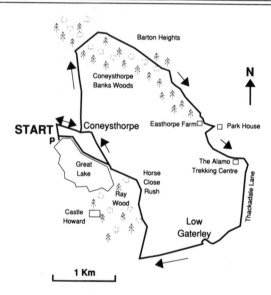

Walk to the nearby road junction and turn right to the neat looking estate village of Coneysthorpe. Turn left along the road through the village and continue straight ahead along a signposted footpath that goes down to a stream. Cross and follow the wide track north. A narrower path continues ahead with a hedge on your left and reaches a track at the edge of Coneysthorpe Banks Woods. Turn left for a short distance. A sharp turn right along a wide track followed by a narrow bridleway, maintaining direction upwards and ignoring other paths, takes you to a wide track on the northern edge of the ridge. This can be muddy. The ridge is followed to Park House.

     Turn right, cross the bridleway to Appleton and bear right. After passing through an open field on your left, a stile is reached before Park House. Bear right and follow the fence to the left. Cross a stile and walk down the drive to the road. The bridleway opposite bears left on a clear track through grass before turning right and downhill. Take a track off to the left which passes between Spring Wood and a small group of trees. Continue south-easterly along the side of the wood and through The Alamo Trekking Centre and turn right at the junction on to Thackadale Lane, another track. Again turn right at the next junction, to reach Low Gaterley. Follow the estate road west to approach Castle Howard (*see* Walk 36). The Mausoleum is seen beyond trees on your right.

Note the Pyramid ahead and to the left before leaving the road to turn right along a wide track down to New River Bridge across the well planted pond. Bear left to the foot of The Temple and pick up a track north along Ray Wood side. This bears left and goes through a gate and between trees to reach another track. Turn left and go along it, approaching the Great Lake, to Coneysthorpe. A short walk left along the road returns you to your car. You may then like to add on a short stroll along the north-eastern side of the lake which is often thronged with anglers.

REFRESHMENTS:
Available in Malton and the inns at Welburn and Appleton are useful.

Walk 54   **NUNNINGTON**   8m (13km)

Maps: OS Sheets Landranger 100; Pathfinder SE 67/77.
A pleasant walk with good views and riverside sections.
Start: At 669783 on Caukleys Bank, near Hovingham.

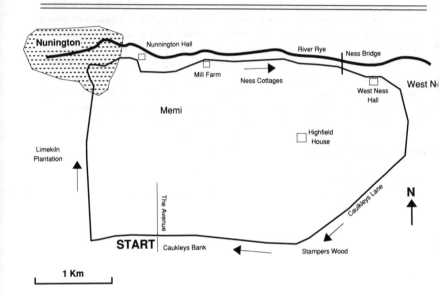

The walk starts from the top of the bank. Leave the road through a gate to the west and walk along the ridge until you reach a group of conifers on the left. Turn right on to a good track which will take you into Nunnington. Take the road down the hill through the village, passing the church and the pub. Continue along the village street until you reach the junction with the main road. In front of you is **Nunnington Hall** with a fine view over the bridge towards it.

Continue up the hill towards the avenue and turn left at the end of the post and rail fence along an access road to a private house. Look for the footpath sign. Turn right there and go over the stile. Turn left with more views of the Hall. At the end of the large garden wall go over a stile, bear slightly left and cross a field heading towards the weir. The path now goes along a dry dyke towards a gate south of the farmhouse. Pass through the gate and into the farmyard. With the mill on your left, go between the buildings through a gate and into an arable field. The walk now follows the river, except where the river loops. There it continues in a more or less straight line with the river and trees on the left.

Follow the path through arable and grass fields until you reach the Welburn to Ness road. Turn right over the bridge and follow the road through the hamlet, past the pumping station until a road is reached. Cross the road and follow the green track uphill and round to the right. Once the ridge is reached, from where there are panoramic views over Ryedale with the Wolds in the distance, you follow a green track back to your start point.

POINTS OF INTEREST:
Nunnington Hall – A National Trust property open to the public. It has an interesting collection of doll's houses.

REFRESHMENTS:
The Royal Oak Inn, Nunnington (tel no: 043 95 271).

Walk 55   RIEVAULX   8m (13km)

Maps: OS Sheets Landranger 100; Outdoor Leisure 26.

Easy going.

Start: At 575850, in the small parking place by the river about 400 yards south of Rievaulx village.

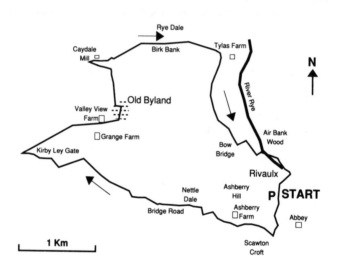

Walk away from the village, by the River Rye, to a T-junction. Turn right, and go over the packhorse bridge towards Scawton. Continue straight on for 1 mile. Just after the road turns sharp left, turn right through a wide entrance, with a finger post signposted for the Cleveland Way and an acorn. Go through the gate and follow the forest track past three large ponds, originally the fish ponds for **Rievaulx Abbey**. The name is pronounced 'ree-vo'. These ponds are home for a colony of ducks.

Follow the track through a gate and continue for 1¹/₂ miles (paths up side valleys are to be ignored) to a tarmac road. Turn right and follow it to **Old Byland**. Go through the village, turn left, then right on a road marked 'Unsuitable for Motor Vehicles'. The road descends steeply into lovely Caydale. Just before a row of tall Scots Pines above Caydale Mill, turn right through a gate. Go forward along the hillside. Look for a bridleway sign, and follow its direction, keeping parallel with the beck. Another bridleway sign is passed. Go forward through a gate to a track through a conifer plantation. This can be muddy in wet weather. The track descends to emerge in open country near Tylas Farm.

Now follow the tarmacked lane away from the farm until it descends steeply to a stream. At the far side go through the gate on the left, cross the field to the riverside and walk downstream. The path goes through a wood in which there are boardwalks and wooden steps. After crossing the stile out of the wood, keep straight on to reach a rough lane. Turn left along the lane, cross over Bow Bridge, and continue to where the lane brings you out to the top end of Rievaulx village. Turn right and walk along the road to your starting point.

POINTS OF INTEREST:

Rievaulx Abbey – The Abbey was the first large Cistercian church to be built in England. The ruins and village are set in a beautiful valley. Rievaulx Terrace, set above the Abbey, has $^1/_2$ mile of lawn and two classical temples.

Old Byland – The monks who came here were disturbed by the bells of Rievaulx, so they moved to the present site of Byland Abbey.

REFRESHMENTS:

The market town of Helmsley is 3 miles distant, with a variety of inns and cafés.
The Crown Hotel in the Market Place (tel no: 0439 70297) is recommended for high teas .

Walk 56   CLAY BANK   8m (13km)

Maps: OS Sheets Landranger 93; Outdoor Leisure 26.

A fine, mainly moorland walk with some climbing.

Start: At 574036, the Clay Bank car park.

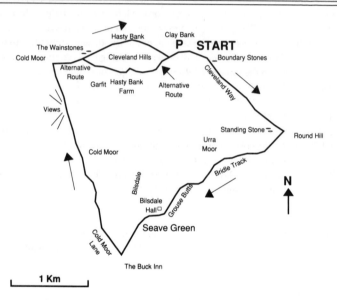

Go left along the road for 200 yards, then turn left through a gate signposted 'Cleveland Way'. Continue along an uphill path, close to a forestry boundary wall on your left and go through a gate. Cross rising ground to a narrow cleft in a rocky outcrop ahead. Scramble up it and continue to a gate where there are notices about lambing and upland nesting birds. Once through it continue in a south-easterly direction along with the Lyke Wake Walk route on a broad track climbing steadily along a cairned way for $1^1/_2$ miles to a boundary stone marked 'M', near a blank notice board on your left. From here a short extension will bring you to a white trig point at the summit of Round Hill on Bottom Head which, at 1491 ft above sea level, is the highest point on the North York Moors. At the boundary stone go right past a large cairn along a broad track south westwards over **Urra Moor** for 2 miles to the moor's edge. After $1^1/_2$ miles you pass a row of shooting butts and, just beyond them, a plaque to the Newton Tower Estate and then a signpost 'To Blowith Crossing'. Where the track turns left go straight ahead, off the moor, with excellent views of Bilsdale for company. Pass a large estate notice on your right, then cross a stile in the wall ahead and continue downhill, passing a ruined barn, also on your right. Follow the stiled bridleway to Bilsdale Hall, where you turn left along a lane to Seave Green. Turn right up signposted and cobbled Cold Moor Lane, past the Wesleyan Chapel. After $^1/_2$ mile leave the lane through a gate and continue northwards over Cold Moor for $2^1/_2$ miles. From this ridge walk, which follows a broad, cairned track, there are superb views into lonely Raisdale and to the Cleveland Hills ahead. At the summit of Cold Moor (1317ft) turn right and go steeply down to Garfit Gap and through a wooden gate at the bottom. Continue through gaps in two walls then steeply uphill to the well known rocky outcrop of The Wainstones. From here panoramic views unfold like the petals of an opening rose. However, if the steep climb is off-putting, take the alternative, slighter longer route, which bypasses The Wainstones by forking right, by going over a stile, as you approach the second wall gap, and taking a path through stiled fields, passing Garfit and Hasty Bank farms. It will bring you to the B1275, where you turn left for 200 yards to Hasty Bank car park. The main route continues past The Wainstones over Hasty Bank along a well-worn track which descends steeply to the B1275. Turn left along it for 200 yards to Hasty Bank car park and the end of a super walk.

POINTS OF INTEREST:
Urra Moor – From here the retrospective views of Gingle Moor, Cold Moor and Hasty Bank are very impressive. From the gate leading from the B1275 to the standing stone on Urra Moor this walk is shared with The Cleveland Way, the Lyke Wake Walk and the Coast to Coast route.

REFRESHMENTS:
There is a tea hut at Clay Bank car park.
The Buck Inn, Chop Gate (tel no: 0642 778334). Coffee, bar meals and sandwiches are also available. It is well placed, half way round the walk.

Walk 57   BILSDALE   9m (14.5km)

Maps: OS Sheets Landranger 100; Outdoor Leisure 26.

Field paths and moorland tracks predominate on this lovely walk. The moorland sections are exposed.

Start: The Newgate Bank car park.

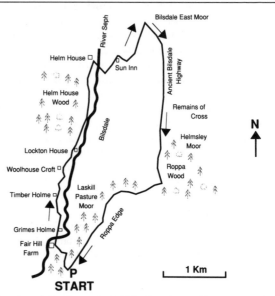

Leave the car park going right along the B1275 for about 300 yards, this section coinciding with the first part of the 29 miles Bilsdale Circuit. Turn left down a signposted path, crossing a stile beside a plantation. At the corner of the plantation continue down a field, crossing two signposted stiles and a farm track. Do not cross the stile close to Fair Hill Farm. Instead, turn right along the field, then turn left through a gate, then right to where a signpost points to the left-hand side gate of two. Continue along the side of the next field bearing left to cross a footbridge over the River Seph. Continue along a green track, veering left to cross a ladder-stile and then turning right along a track. Pass two barns, and as the Bilsdale Circuit turns left, uphill, go straight ahead on a track to Timber Holme Farm. The obvious path beyond the farm building is private, so cross a corner stile to a woodland path. Keep to the path beyond the wood to reach the Laskgill-Hawnby road. Go left to where it bifurcates and take the right-hand road to Lockton House. Just beyond the farm turn right through a gate with a blue arrow and follow similar arrows along a muddy bridleway. Go ahead through gated fields and by Belman Bank Wood, turning left, uphill, alongside it and leaving it through a corner gap in a wall. Go north along an enclosed track, beyond which the route can be muddy. Nearing Helm House go through a white gate, right, between barns, and cross a field to a gate. Turn right along a farm road, crossing the River Seph, to reach the B1275. Go left as far as the Sun Inn on your right. Turn right between it and the original Sun Inn, now called Spout House. Go through a gated farmyard, then left by a byre and through a gate. Turn sharp right, passing a barn on your right. Go through another gate and up a field to a stile. Cross and go half-left heading for a gate in the top corner of the field leading to Bilsdale East Moor. Go left along the rutted track that edges the moor for $1/2$ mile until a wooden gate is seen on the left. Just before the gate turn half-right and head south, through heather, for about 1 mile to where a fire break cuts across your line of walk. Keep going south on an undefined route towards a row of grouse butts. Past butt No 8 the route is parallel to a sunken, heather-covered gully, the old Bilsdale road to Magna Via on Roppa Edge. Further south are the remains of two crosses on your left, the second of which is Roppa Cross. As you move southwards the path becomes better defined. After a mile, at the edge of Roppa Wood, the Bilsdale Circuit is rejoined. Cross a stile and take a sandy track to where it turns left. There go right, uphill beside a plantation, climbing steeply to the forest drive below Roppa Edge. Go right through a gate and immediately left up Rievaulx Bank, climbing steadily to Roppa Edge, from where there is a magnificent panorama embracing both the Howardian and the Cleveland Hills. It is well worth all the energy used to get there. To complete the walk turn right and go along a broad, level track for 2 miles back to Newgate Bank car park.

REFRESHMENTS:

The Sun Inn, Bilsdale (tel no: 04396 206). No meals provided but you can eat your own food there.

Walk 58   HOVINGHAM   10m (16km)

Maps: OS Sheets Landranger 100; Pathfinder SE 67/77.

A walk through the gentle and pleasant Howardian Hills. Often on good tracks, but can become a little muddy in parts.

Start: In the village of Hovingham.

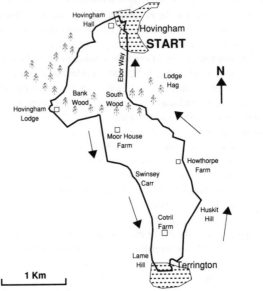

Walk north past the entry to Hovingham Hall entrance and the church, and bear right down Churchside. Cross the footbridge, turn left along Brookside and follow the road right along the **Ebor Way**. A stile is reached on the left. Cross and follow the field side, crossing two more stiles. Bear left to a gate and a track to a bridge and the road. There are good views of the Hall on this section. Turn right along the road and then take a signposted track that bears left through woodland with a stream on the left. Cross this near a corner of the wood on the left. Maintain direction, keeping a fence on your left. Bear right to a gate and, shortly, a track. Turn left and follow the track past Hovingham Lodge. When the track, now tarmacked, turns right, turn left downhill, with the hedge on your right. Cross a footbridge and continue uphill, diverting through a field on the left if the way becomes overgrown. Turn right when you reach the road.

124

Where the road bends to the right take the bridleway by the farm entry. Go left diagonally across a field to a gate. This should be clear, but if not you could use the tractor route round. Make your way through two more fields to join a pleasant track which takes you into **Terrington**. The track passes Swinsey Carr Wood and Rose Cottage Farm, and Low Water Lake is seen through the trees. Walk ahead and left past the Bay Horse Inn and turn left by the church. Carry straight on up to the school field and turn right. Follow the clear path across the next field and then turn north to follow field boundaries, bearing right up to a footbridge. Cross and maintain direction up to a track. Turn left and continue ahead where a bridleway joins from the right. The track goes through Howthorpe Farm and downhill to a wood. Turn left along the field to a stile and gate. Cross a stream and turn right along the diverted path. This follows the edge of a wood and a stream up to a narrow belt of trees. Go a little left on a path through overgrowth then right to enter the next field. Continue to a small gate and cross the footbridge ahead to reach a gate into Lodge Hag. Take the track uphill. Ignore all tracks to the side as you walk north-westerly to emerge from the wood. Walk downhill using a footpath to the left of the junction to reach the start.

POINTS OF INTEREST:
The Ebor Way – Is a 70 miles route from Helmsley to Ilkley.
Terrington – A fine village on a ridge of the Howardian Hills.

REFRESHMENTS:
The Bay Horse, (tel no: 065384 255). Open Monday–Friday 7–11pm, Friday 11–2.30pm, Saturday 11–3pm and 5.30–11pm and Sunday 12–3pm and 7–10.30pm.

Walk 59 **STOKESLEY** 10m (16km)

Maps: OS Sheets Landranger 93; Pathfinder NZ 40/50 & 41/51.
*An easy level walk along the banks of the River Leven and across
well waymarked field paths.*
Start: Stokesley.

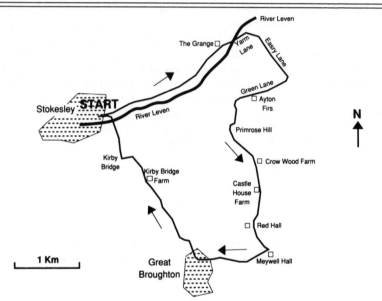

Leave Stokesley, a quiet market town, along its High Street to the roundabout at
its eastern end. Turn left along Springfield for 50 yards to where a footpath sign on
the right points along an enclosed path to the A172. Cross it, go over the stile on the
other side and continue straight ahead over stiled fields to the River Leven. Turn left
along the river bank and opposite the sewage works, where the path has been diverted,
turn left near a fenced field's edge, then right across a white railed footbridge over
a drainage channel to rejoin the river. Continue over a stile, away from the river,
crossing a field on your left and going over another stile. Keep going roughly
eastwards, crossing more stiles, to pass The Grange before reaching Yarm Lane. Go
right along it to **Great Ayton**.

Opposite The Garth cross the River Leven on a white footbridge and go over the

A172. Go along Mill Lane to Easy Lane and southwards along it for 1 mile. Just past a road sign turn right along Green Lane for $^1/_2$ mile, passing behind Ayton Firs Farm. Go through a green gate, walking westwards along the edge of two fields, to join a cart-track near an ash tree. Turn left and follow the track southward, following yellow arrows, to join the Easby Road. Turn right along it, passing a boundary stone on your right and where you see the signs for Crow Wood and Primrose Hill Farms turn left along an unsurfaced bridle road for about $1^1/_2$ miles. You will pass Primrose Hill Farm on your left and then cross Broughton Beck. The way is now uphill and roughly southwards, passing Crow Wood Farm on your left, Castle House Farm on your right and then crossing a dismantled railway to reach the Ingleby Greenhough Road. Turn right over a beck and take the signposted path on your left past Red Hall, right. Continue through white gates past Chapelgarth on your right, following the yellow arrows. They will direct you across a stile in the facing fence and over two more stiles. Go over a beck, across another stile, up a wood and across a field towards Meywell Hall, where you turn right. Pass the Hall on your left and go over stiled fields to Great Broughton. Turn right along Great Broughton High Street to reach the crossroads. Turn left along Kirby Road to a signposted path on your right. Continue north, over two fields, then bear half left near the narrow end of a field. Cross a stile and go right along a large cultivated field to exit through a gap and re-cross the disused railway. Cross another stile and continue along the edge of a field, passing Kirby Bridge Farm on your right. The way is now across a gravel road and alongside some buildings on the right. Between the end of a hedge and some bushes cross a stile and go left with the hedge on your left to a corner stile. Continue along a hedge on your right and where it ends go half left, diagonally across another field and across a stile to the flood relief channel of Eller Beck. Turn left along the embankment to Kirby Bridge where you turn right along Kirby Road back into Stokesley.

POINTS OF INTEREST:

Great Ayton – A monument made of granite from Point Hicks, Australia marks the spot of Captain Cook's cottage. The cottage was exported to Australia in 1934. Captain Cook's Monument and Roseberry Topping are both clearly seen from the walk.

REFRESHMENTS:

There are pubs in Stokesley, Great Ayton and Great Broughton.

Walk 60   CLAY BANK AREA   10m (16km)

Maps: OS Sheets Landranger 93 & 100; Outdoor Leisure 26.

Woodland, moorland and farm track walking, with 1100 feet of climbing.

Start: At 573035, the Clay Bank car park.

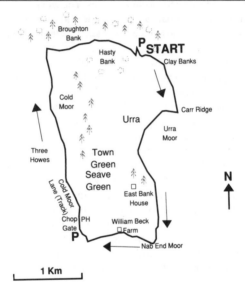

Go left from the car park following the main road for 100 yards to reach a timber 'bee-hive' litter bin and a narrow gate on your left. Go through and follow the path uphill, with a wall to the left. After $\frac{1}{4}$ mile pass through a second gate and continue uphill through a narrow cleft in the rocky outcrop on the nose of Carr Ridge. Further on pass through the final narrow gate on to the moor. Turn right within yards of the moor gate and follow a bridleway which contours along the ancient earthworks – known as Cromwells Trenches. This path is well-defined even in late summer when the heather and bracken are deep. After $\frac{1}{2}$ mile drop down in and out of a small valley which is the head of Bilsdale Beck. Continue for almost a mile and cross a moorland access track at Medd Crag.

From the access track the route becomes less well-defined. Carry on contouring around the valley, the ancient earthworks acting as a good guide, taking you up a slight climb to where the route becomes clear again on the moor edge above East Bank Plantation. After about a mile you will see an intake (moorland field) wall ahead of you. Follow the uphill edge of this to a gate where you leave the moor and go downhill to William Beck Farm. Turn left at the farm buildings and follow the farm track to the main road. Go right and follow the road for $^1/_4$ mile passing the Chop Gate (pronounced Chop Yat) village hall car park and the Buck Inn on your left.

A hundred yards further, to the left, is a minor road to Raisedale. A path leads up behind a house almost in front of you, becoming Cold Moor Lane, and continues through trees and shrubs for almost $^1/_2$ mile to where it ends at a moor gate. Two miles of bridleway take you upwards past Three Howes to the top of Cold Moor. This view ahead is spectacular at night, illuminated from Scotch Corner in the north west, through Darlington, Teesside Airport, Stockton, Middlesbrough, Hartlepool – about 30 miles of lighting!

Turn right at the top of Cold Moor. You are now again on the route of several long distance walks. Go downhill through a gate hole and upwards to the Wainstones, a local climbing area. To the left-hand side of the needle outcrop a rocky, but easy, path goes up through a gully to the moor top.

Continue around the northern escarpment of the moor top for a mile. To your left is Roseberry Topping, Cleveland's Matterhorn, and to its right is Easby Moor with the monument to Captain Cook who was a local man. (**Captain Cook Museums** can be found in Middlesbrough, Whitby and Great Ayton.)

A path descends from the moor top down to the forest track, near to the seat in memory of 'Robbie' who died on the Lyke Wake Walk. Turn right after going over the stile near the memorial seat and follow the forest track downhill, back to the road near the car park.

POINTS OF INTEREST:
Captain Cook Museums – Birthplace, Middlesbrough (tel no: 0642 311211), Cook Memorial Museum, Whitby (tel no: 0947 601900), Captain Cook Schoolroom Museum, village green, Great Ayton.

REFRESHMENTS:
The Buck Inn, Chop Gate (tel no: 0642 778334).

Walk 61　　　**BATTERSBY**　　　14m (22.5km)

Maps: OS Sheets Landranger 93 & 94; Outdoor Leisure 26.
A good mix of woodland, moorland and field walking.
Start: At 594062, Bank Foot Farm.

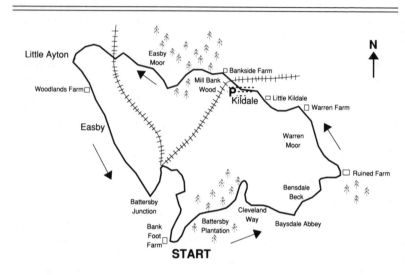

1 Km

Climb the broad track into Park Plantation where, after 100 yards, go left along a clear
track, first following a contour, then climbing steadily. After $1^1/_2$ miles turn right, where
a clear track intersects, climbing steeply. Continue along it as it levels out and bends
to the right, doubling back on the original track at a much higher level. Soon the way
veers to the left and out of the plantation on to open moor. Continue across the moor
on a clear path to join the Baysdale road where it turns sharp left to go downhill to
Baysdale. Go down the hill, between the buildings of Baysdale Abbey, (now a farm)
and left to continue close to Baysdale Beck, left, for $^3/_4$ mile. Where the road bends right
at a farm building go left over a bridge into a field and right, across it, to a gate. Beyond
a clear track leads uphill close to a wall, right, to a ruinous farmhouse. Turn left up a
paddock to a corner gate with a delapidated building to the right of it. Once through the
gate go to the rear of the building where a bridleway sign points to a clear track crossing

the moor. The track goes north-west past a cairn at the summit and another bridleway sign beyond, crossing out of Baysdale and over Warren Moor into a shallow valley, where you cross the infant River Leven. Continue on a winding track to Warren House Farm, seen clearly ahead. Passing to the left of the farm follow the road left through a plantation, downhill, through Little Kildale and on to Kildale. Turn right at a junction and right again along a road under a railway bridge. Go uphill as far as Bankside Farm, right, and cross a stile on the left. Go along a forest ride, and when it forks take the right-hand fork, climbing steadily through Millbank Wood. Once clear of trees, turn right, uphill, for a few yards to a gap in the wall on your left leading to Easby Moor. Following a defined path, cross the moor on a contour and go through a wicket gate into another, small plantation. Beyond it go left and downhill. Bear right along the clear path at the bottom of which go through a white painted gate to cross the railway line. Enter a field and cross it with a hedge on your right. Turn right when the hedge does and continue down a farm road into Little Ayton. Cross the bridge over the River Leven at the end of the village and continue along the road for $^1/_4$ mile to a signposted stile in the fence on your left. Cross and bear left to a gate with a waymarker. Go through and immediately turn right. Follow waymarkers close to the river past Woodhouse Farm, left, and continue to Easby. Beyond turn left at a junction for 100 yards, then right to Pilly Hall Farm. Still following waymarkers continue over fields, southerly, to a farm ahead. Keep to the left of it, as the arrows indicate, and continue over fields, with the hedge to your left, to Battersby Junction. Just short of the railway station turn left and go along the edge of a field at the far end of which go left for a few yards and through a clear gap on your right. Continue under the railway underpass into a pasture and go diagonally left to a footbridge. Cross it and the stile just ahead, slightly to your right. Once over the stile continue left up the side of a field and turn right at the end of it to a farm. Cross a stile on your left (between outbuildings and the farmhouse) and proceed to the road. Go right at the junction, over Otter Hill's Beck. After $^1/_4$ mile, where the road bends sharply right, go through a signposted gateway into a field on the left and cross it diagonally to the far right-hand corner. Continue with a fence on the left down a second field, turning right at the bottom of it. Continue close to the left fence to a bridge over a dyke. Cross and turn right, and immediately go through a gate into a large field and take the broad track to Bank Foot Farm, seen in the distance.

POINTS OF INTEREST:

When Baysdale Abbey was built, a nearby beck was bridged. Today's bridge, which carries the road looks nondescript, but from the riverbank the transformation is magical. The arch is Norman, possibly 12th century, and very beautiful.

Walk 62   **YORK BAR WALLS**   3m (5km)

Map: None required

A walk around the Walls surrounding the City of York, with splendid views and numerous opportunities for deviations.

Start: Anywhere on the Bar Walls, though the description starts at Monk Bar.

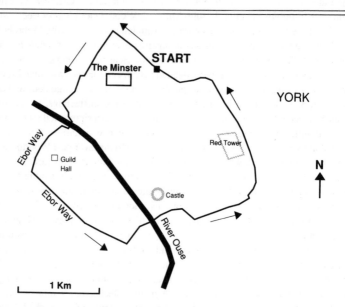

Inside the Walls climb the staircase on the left of the Bar, to your left you will see York Minster and buildings and gardens in the Minster surrounds, including Treasurer's House (open to public). To your right you can see the College of Ripon and St John's.

The Walls turns left and you are now on the northern side of the City (Monk Bar was the eastern gate). Soon you come to Bootham Bar – notice the portcullis on your right.

After leaving the Bar cross the road towards the Art Gallery, and take the path to the left of King Manor (behind the bus shelter). This leads you into the gardens surrounding the Yorkshire Museum.

At the T-junction of paths turn left and then second right. Follow the sign for toilets and turn right through the iron fence to the River Ouse.

Turn left, climb the steps and cross the river. At the other side of the bridge turn right on to the Walls.

The Walls soon turn left again and you are now on the western side of the City. The next gate is Micklegate Bar, the only Bar open to the public.

When the Walls again turn left you are on the southern edge of the City. The mound to your left used to carry one of two towers which guarded the River Ouse. You will shortly see the other, Cliffords Tower, which is open to the public.

After leaving the Walls, cross the zebra crossing and the river. Follow the road and cross the River Foss before crossing the road to rejoin the Walls behind the Rectangular Tower.

You are now back on the east side of the Walls. This side is in two sections as there was no need for a continuous wall, the middle area being an impenetrable swamp.

When you leave the first section, follow the road and turn left at the next bridge over the river. Cross the road and rejoin the Walls. On this section look out for the ice house over the wall to your right.

Soon you return to the start point at Monk Bar, which is, at present, a Picture Gallery.

POINTS OF INTEREST:
Too numerous to list.

REFRESHMENTS:
Many to choose from.

Walk 63   **TADCASTER**   6m (9.5km)

Maps: OS Sheets Landranger 105; Pathfinder SE 44/54.

Gentle walking along good tracks and field paths in pleasant countryside. Can be muddy in parts in wet conditions.

Start: The main car park on the eastern bank of the River Wharfe in Tadcaster.

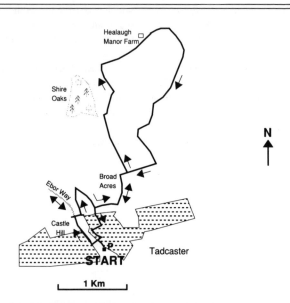

Cross the road and the bridge and immediately turn right along the riverside path to **St Helen's Church**. Divert to see the church and churchyard before returning to the path and continuing towards the bottom of the old railway viaduct. Cross the stile on the left immediately before it and climb the steps to the top. Turn right and cross. Turn sharp right and descend the steps to the east bank of the river. Again turn right underneath the viaduct and cross a stile. Walk a short distance along the riverside before bearing right, uphill, to a stile. Continue uphill to a stile in the far right-hand corner of the field and cross into Wighill Lane. Turn right and walk along the roadside path to reach a modern estate on the left. Turn left along the track between the newer and older house before the estate. The lane bears left, past a house and pond, and then it turns right by some

134

houses including Broad Acres. Turn left at the track junction at this point.

Reach woodland on the right and the tip of **Shire Oaks Wood** on the left. Later the track turns right to pass **Healaugh Manor Farm**. Continue ahead along the rougher track. A series of ponds on the left provide a haven for wildlife. Near them the track turns right. As the main track turns left towards Healaugh, walk straight ahead on the narrower track to reach an open field. Bear half right across this cropped field towards the left-hand edge of the centre of three small woods. In some circumstances, it may prove easier to use the field boundary to the right. Reach the River Foss and follow the well-used river path southwards. Reach a footbridge over the Foss and bear left to the right-hand corner of the small wood. Turn left by the side of the wood and then right towards another wood. Pass through a gap in the hedge before the wood into the adjacent field. Reach the wood and turn left alongside it. Reach a small gate and a bridge over a drain. Cross and bear half-left across the field to a small gap between a hedge and larger trees. Pass through and turn right by the trees and then turn left along the side of a replanted hedge to reach a track. Turn right and soon retrace your steps along the track to Wighill Lane.

Turn left and cross the road before turning right, downhill, by Rosemary Row. Continue left at the bottom to reach the main road. Cross and turn right, back to the car park.

POINTS OF INTEREST:

The busy and historic town of Tadcaster is a noted centre of the brewing industry. The railway viaduct was never used by a railway, as the latter was never completed! The walk can be extended along the west bank of the Wharfe past the viaduct.

St Helen's Church has traces of its Norman origin. It was once taken down and re-constructed 5ft higher to reduce danger from flooding. An old cross in the churchyard is surmounted by a sundial.

Shire Oaks Wood is the home of a large heronry. Deer are also occasionally seen.

Healaugh Manor Farm – one of two bearing this name. Some fascinating medieval buildings are still visible.

REFRESHMENTS:

Can be obtained from the car park café or from one of the several inns nearby. No refreshments on route.

Walk 64   **YORK**   7m (11km)

Maps: OS Sheets Landranger 105; Pathfinder SE 65/75 & 64/74.
Easy walking through town, along riverside, track and grass path. Almost flat and mostly good underfoot. Flooding possible.
Start: York Minster.

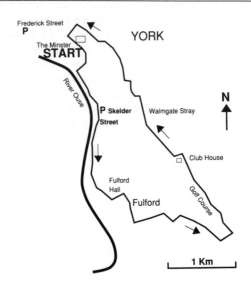

From the Minster walk to Low Petergate and bear right at King's Square into The Shambles. Turn right at Pavement and cross at the junction to Coppergate. At the next junction cross to King Street. Turn left along the bank of the River Ouse, passing the boats at King's Staith. Walk under Skeldergate Bridge and cross the River Foss at Blue Bridge. Through a gate, New Walk goes by the riverside. Where this ends, use the footpath near to the houses or the longer riverside route over a field. Continue ahead, but away from the river, due to a pumping station, along Love Lane footpath. This widens and passes a travellers' camp, St Oswald's Church Hall and crosses the end of St Oswald's Road. Where the lane ends, continue ahead along the clear footpath away from the river. Reach a wire fence and stile. Cross and turn left down the brick walled Fulford Lane.

Turn right along the busy Fulford Road and cross at the 'pelican'. At the main road junction turn left down Germany Lane, a track, passing in front of Fulford Mews. This turns right, left at a junction and right again, to reach a field near the A64. Bear right a little way into the field to reach the edge of a wood. Cross a stile and turn left along the roadside grass verge. In the absence of a stile, pass under the bridge and gain access to Fulford Golf Course by a little climb up the grassy side of the bridge. Turn right and follow the tarmacked path along the side of the golf course. Pass the clubhouse and use the narrow footpath to Heslington Lane. Cross and turn left. Turn right, through a metal kissing gate on to Walmgate Stray. Walk ahead, across a bridge, and bear left, aiming to the left of the high brick wall surrounding the Retreat. Pass between this and allotments, through gates, to reach Heslington Road. Cross and turn left. Turn right into Wellington Street and along the path, right of the church.

Turn left in Lawrence Street to reach Walmgate Bar. Cross and climb up steps to the City Walls. Walk east and descend at Red Tower. Continue along Foss Islands Road where the wildlife on the Foss compensates for the industrial views. Cross Layerthorpe Bridge and again climb steps up to the Walls. Descend and re-ascend through a tower at Monk Bar. There are excellent views of the Minster and the surrounding buildings before you reach Bootham Bar. Descend and turn left to the Minster.

POINTS OF INTEREST:
Too numerous to mention.

REFRESHMENTS:
A wide variety of refreshment is readily available in the city.

Walk 65   **FISHLAKE**   7m (11km)

Maps: OS Sheets Landranger 111; Pathfinder SE 61/71.
Very gentle walking mainly along pleasant green lanes.
Start: The Church, Fishlake.

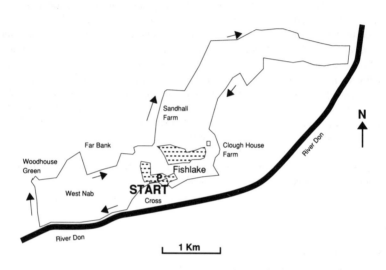

Walk westwards along Main Street noting an old cross. At the end of a small green, turn left along a footpath which quickly bears right behind houses and to the rear of the Old Anchor Inn. Cross stiles and a brick bridge and cross the flood embankment to reach the bank on the River Don. On the opposite bank Stainforth Colliery appears to be quite close, but will not be seen for very long. Where the gap between river and embankment narrows, cross over the latter to reach a stile. Cross and walk a little way ahead to a road junction. Turn right, along Moss Road, and reach Woodhouse Green Farm on the left. Turn right through a gate and bear a little right on to an embankment at the side of a pond. Walk along the left-hand side of this and a second pond to reach Barnsbridge Farm. Continue ahead to a cross tracks. Turn right and, soon, left at a junction to go along a wide grass track which leads to Trundle Lane in Fishlake. There is the stump of an old cross here. Turn right along the road, cross and turn left down Eastfield Lane.

Pass the first field on the right and turn right, through a gap in the hedge, along the field side footpath to reach a short track. Walk ahead to Pinfold Lane.

Turn left along the pavement, passing the cricket ground and Park Farm. Shortly, cross and turn right along a track immediately past a house. The track bears left, passes Sandhall Farm and continues to reach a road. Turn right and go straight ahead along a track at the road corner. Turn right at a track T-junction. The track quickly turns left, past a small pond, and reaches the embankment of the River Don. Turn right and reach the road to Fishlake close to the river bridge. Turn right before reaching a junction and then turn left towards Fishlake. At the next junction, just before Clough House Farm, bear left along the footpath over a footbridge and a stile into a field. Keep right. Cross and follow the enclosed path to the road. Cross the road and, a little to the right, cross a stile. Take the centre, enclosed, path along an embankment to reach and turn right along the River Don embankment. Reach **Fishlake** and turn right, along the side of **St Cuthbert's Church**, to reach Church Street and the start.

POINTS OF INTEREST:

Fishlake – Is a small, quite pleasant village with some historical interest. The names of some of the village roads will arouse interest.

St Cuthbert's Church – Has a nicely carved entrance, and retains a Norman window and font.

Walk 66   STAMFORD BRIDGE   7m (11km)

Maps: OS Sheets Landranger 105; Pathfinder SE 65/75.

A gentle stroll, much over grass field paths, and along the tree-lined banks of the River Derwent.

Start: The car park at Stamford Bridge.

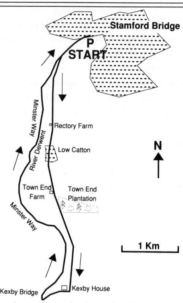

Walk to the river and follow the path south along the river bank below the disused railway bridge. Reach a fence ahead and bear a little left to a stile. Beyond the path continues between a hedge on your left and a wire fence: after the next stile, the hedge is on your right. Maintain direction, walking past a small plantation. Pass through a gate and walk slightly uphill along the fence side and, at the corner, keep ahead across an open field. Rectory Farm and the unusually shaped All Saint's Church are passed on your right as you reach a stile and the road at Low Catton by the Old Rectory. Walk through the village, past the Gold Cup Inn, and along open road to Town End Farm where the road bends. Take the bridleway on the right, which passes through a gate and along a wide grass track across a field. After a second gate keep straight ahead with the hedge on your left. The river is briefly close by here. Pass through a small gate near buildings and walk along the hedgeside to a stile and gate. Follow the track past the side of Kexby House to the A1079. Turn right along the footpath by the side of this busy road, past the front of the house, and go down to the road bridge at Kexby. Note the older road bridge.

Immediately across the bridge turn right, over a stile, and follow the mainly grass field path along the riverside across a series of stiles. As you pass Scoreby Manor House Farm, do not use the gate, crossing, instead, the less obvious stile slightly downhill to the right. The path then continues across a rougher, slightly overgrown area, still close to the river. The path quickly becomes easier as Low Catton is passed and, before long, you again pass under the old railway bridge and walk over the narrow old main road bridge. Cross the road and use the footbridge on the left. A notice will remind you that you are re-entering the well loved East Riding of Yorkshire County rather than the less popular administrative area of Humberside. The car park at **Stamford Bridge** is then on the opposite side, but it is worthwhile diverting ahead to have a quick look at the pleasant area at the north side of The Square, above a mill stream.

POINTS OF INTEREST:

Stamford Bridge – Close by is the site of the battle fought in 1066 in which King Harold defeated Harald and his Viking and Shetlander army, perhaps leaving him a little weaker to fight at Hastings. Imagine the many longboats as you walk along the river. The small town is very busy but retains some charm.

REFRESHMENTS:

Plentiful with three inns and several cafés, apart from the Corn Mill Restaurant, within a small area at Stamford Bridge, and the Bridge Hotel restaurant at Kexby.

Walk 67   ACASTER SELBY   7m (11km)

Maps: OS Sheets Landranger 105; Pathfinder SE 44/54.

Gentle walking along tracks, field paths and riverside through pleasant countryside.

Start: The church of St John's in Acaster Selby.

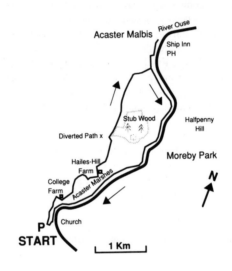

Walk northwards along the road, noting a large clock on the wall of a building, and passing Manor Farm. Where the road turns left, go right along the very short stretch of road to College Farm. This reaches a track which turns to the left and round the right-hand side of a barn. Follow the track to the left of the low College Hill. It soon bears right and reaches a line of trees, then continues towards Hailes Hill Farm with the hedge now on the right-hand side.

On reaching the farm do not enter, but turn left along a track and, at the end of the line of trees, turn right by the side of a fence and keep ahead on to the old perimeter track of the disused Acaster Airfield. Follow the track bearing slightly right and later left, until it nears a gate entry into Stub Wood. Turn right and enter the wood. Take the right-hand track of two. In a few yards, a short stretch of tarmac goes to the left. Just before this, turn left along the narrow and not always very distinct path meandering a little through the wood to reach a stile. Go over into an open field and cross to a small section of wooden fencing across a gap in the hedge opposite. Continue to bear very slightly right across the next field and slightly left across that following. Aim almost ahead towards the right-hand corner of a hedge and cross the nearby stile. Walk ahead with the hedge on your right, and then pass to the left of a small pond. Cross the footbridge near to a gate and walk along the right-hand side of a large and well maintained pond on which several species of wildfowl are usually to be seen. Pass through a wooden gate and walk through the right-hand side of a boatyard. Cross a stile by the side of a gate and reach the road at **Acaster Malbis**.

Turn right along the road past The Manor. The road turns left. It is easy to extend the walk by continuing along the road and taking the signed footpath to the riverside and turning left to the Ship Inn. Return to the road corner. From here go straight ahead on a track. This turns left and reaches the footpath by the side of the River Ouse. This can be easily followed right back to St John's Church, **Acaster Selby**. Naburn Lock and Moreby Hall with its parkland on the opposite bank is passed. Walk round the church and follow the short path back to the road.

POINTS OF INTEREST:

Acaster Malbis – Can become busy with fishermen and boating enthusiasts and there can be much activity on the river.

Acaster Selby – A very small and quiet village. The church is pleasantly set in a riverside field. The 'no through road' ensures little traffic.

REFRESHMENTS:

The Ship Inn, Acaster Malbis (tel no: 0904 705609).

Walk 68   NETHER POPPLETON   8m (13km)

Maps: OS Sheets Landranger 105; Pathfinder SE 45/55.

Gentle walking along field paths and tracks and riverside. A little woodland.

Start: The northern corner of Nether Poppleton.

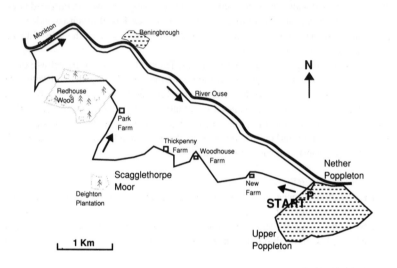

Leave your car at the small open space at the edge of a little woodland close to the River Ouse. Just to the south-west a stile by a gate gives access to the footpath along the field boundary towards New Farm. The path changes over to the left-hand side of the hedge and reaches a gate at the farm. Pass through, keep to the right of the main building and go through a gate on the right. Turn left along a drain side and follow around the field side to a stile. Continue ahead to a second stile and on to a track. Turn right and walk to the derelict Woodhouse Farm, turning left in front of it to a gate. Cross straight over the field to a gate and a bridge over The Foss, a small stream. Continue left of the hedge and past a new house. Turn right through the next gate after that to the house entry. An indistinct grass track follows the fence ahead going round the field corner. Go through a gate to the left of Thickpenny Farm. Join the farm road and walk along this as it passes to the right of Deighton Plantation and reaches a private road but public bridleway, by a house.

Turn right at this junction to walk past the neatly maintained Park Farm and Redhouse Wood. A short cut is allowed through the wood, but the right of way follows the road along the edge of the wood and around its corner. The entry to Red House School is past, then just before the road bears right, turn left through a gate into the wood. Walk through the wood along the wide right-hand track, keeping straight ahead at all junctions. Immediately before the far edge of the wood is reached, a smaller path goes a little to the right to reach a stile. Follow the field boundary right and left round the corner to reach a stile in the next corner. Cross over the grass ahead and go slightly downhill to reach the bank of the River Nidd. The small village of Moor Monkton can be reached by turning left, but has little to make a diversion very worthwhile.

Turn right and follow the bank of the Nidd to its confluence with the River Ouse opposite the pretty looking village of Nun Monkton. Walk along the river bank back to Nether Poppleton passing through a series of gates or crossing stiles. The pleasant parkland of Beningbrough Hall is passed, as well as Beningbrough village on the opposite bank. A modern water extraction station is reached and the path passes between the **River Ouse** and a reservoir. A small diversion away from the river bank and over a footbridge enables us to cross The Foss once more, this time as it runs into the Ouse. The woodland at **Nether Poppleton** is reached where a wide path bears right along a small beck side and back to the car.

POINTS OF INTEREST:

River Ouse – Is navigable along its length, with the help of locks. A few boats are moored along the bank, and others are likely to provide interest as they pass by.

Nether Poppleton – A pleasant suburban village. There is a small war memorial and a village pump. All Saints' Church is fairly close by.

REFRESHMENTS:

Close to the village green in Upper Poppleton are the White Horse Hotel and the Collingwood Arms where refreshment can be obtained.

Walk 69   **BISHOP WILTON**   8m (13km)

Maps: OS Sheets Landranger 106; Pathfinder SE 85/95 & 65/75.

A moderately hilly walk from the edge of the Wolds.

Start: The village of Bishop Wilton.

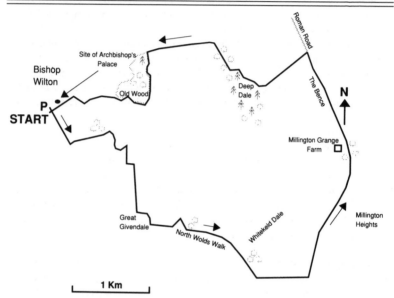

Walk along the road south past the Fleece Inn up to a gate and stile on your left. Enter the rough grass field, which contains many springs, and walk uphill close to the field edge. Turn right, within the field, at the top. A gate, slightly hidden above a mound, is reached. Pass through and over the fence above. Turn right and follow field edges over stiles to reach a small gate. There are good views towards York. Turn left along a track and continue to **Great Givendale**. Turn left along the road to a junction.

    Take the track on the left of the small church and follow this through the valley. Go through two gates with a bridge between and walk straight uphill beyond them. Turn left without crossing the fence reached near Little Givendale Farm, and follow the field edge to a road. A long section of road, not too unpleasant, follows as you turn left uphill to Millington Heights. Millington Wood is passed on the right. Bear left at the junction after Millington Grange Farm. You are now on The Bence, a Roman road. Reach a gate on the left, with a signpost, and follow the track, noting the dale appearing on your left. This quickly deepens and where it starts to open out into its junction with Deepdale, walk downhill, cross stiles at the bottom and follow the footpath uphill to reach a track near a small hut. Turn right, uphill, through woodland. The track reaches a road: cross to the path opposite.

The path leads down to woodland and a path junction. Turn left in front of the wood and after rounding the field corner, cross a stile and follow the field boundary as it goes round the top of a dale. **Bishop Wilton** is seen below. After reaching a field corner and turning left, a small gate and a stile are reached. Continue downhill in the next field, soon bearing left away from the fence and between bushes to reach another small gate. Beware of mud in this section. Cross the next field bearing right downhill to the left of the field corner. Cross a stile, and turn right along a path to re-enter Bishop Wilton.

POINTS OF INTEREST:

Great Givendale – Has some unusual oak-like trees that tend to keep their leaves throughout the winter. The delightful dale itself has a small nature reserve centred around the stream and a pond. Waterfowl, particularly geese can be seen.

Bishop Wilton – Beautifully placed just below the edge of the Wolds, the church spire very prominent. A pleasant small stream runs through the village.

REFRESHMENTS:

The Fleece Inn, Bishop Wilton (tel no: 075 96251) provides good bar meals and has a restaurant.

Walk 70   LONG MARSTON   8m (13km)

Maps: OS Sheets Landranger 105; Pathfinder SE 45/55 & 44/54.

Pleasant, slightly undulating countryside visiting a battlefield.

Start: The crossroads by the Sun Inn, Long Marston.

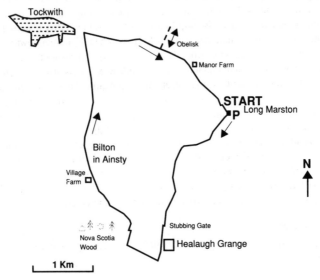

From the crossroads by the Sun Inn walk round the green in Butt Hedge, turning right and then left along a lane to reach the signposted village hall. Continue along the track on the north-west side of the hall and ahead, along the hedge and field side as it curves a little, to reach a tarmacked lane. Turn left along the lane and, where this turns left, bear slightly right along a grass track to reach a bridge over a drain at Stubbing Gate. Cross, turn right and quickly left, uphill, along the narrow path left between cropped fields towards Healaugh Grange Farm. As you reach the farm, bear left and walk between buildings and a line of trees, then along the farm drive, to reach a T-junction.

Turn right along the tarmacked lane to reach a gate at the end. Pass through and turn right, uphill, along a grass track to a gate. Pass through and turn left to reach the edge of Nova Scotia Wood. Turn right and follow the side of the wood to reach a corner where a track goes straight ahead with a hedge on the right. Just before entering Bilton this becomes an enclosed lane, and then a road as you pass the Chequers Inn. Follow this road as it bears left and right to reach the B1224 by the side of **St Helen's Church**. Cross the road and walk along Moor Lane, keeping straight ahead where a track goes left to Bilton Grange farm. The track becomes greener and more open, but it narrows as it follows the side of a drain. It soon widens again and becomes enclosed before it reaches the minor road at the eastern edge of Tockwith.

Turn right, along the road, part of which has a good verge, to reach the **Obelisk**. Just past the next hedge, you can pass through the gate and walk down Moor Lane to reach a small drain. Much of the fighting in the battle of Marston Moor occurred here. Return to the road and continue to the first house in Long Marston. Before the road bends, turn right along a track by the side of a garden of Manor Farm, and turn left by the left-hand side of a building. Pass through a gate and cross a field. Go through another gate and over a second field to reach a third gate. This may be a little obstructed, but pass through, walk to the right of the barn and go along the muddy lane to reach open fields. Keep straight ahead to reach a hedge corner, and follow the left-hand side of the hedge to reach a stile. Cross and turn left to reach the Tockwith road. Turn right to the Sun Inn.

POINTS OF INTEREST:

St Helen's Church – Dates from early Norman times, and though small, is interesting.
Obelisk – Situated close to the centre of the battle of Marston Moor, 2 July 1644, in which Cromwell finally defeated the Royalist forces led by Prince Rupert. Note the hill on the opposite side of the road, Cromwell's Plump.

REFRESHMENTS:

These can be obtained from either of the two inns on the route, or from one of the inns in Tockwith.

Walk 71   BUBWITH – ROUTE 1   8m (13km)

Maps: OS Sheets Landranger 105; Pathfinder SE 63/73.
Very flat along riverside, disused railway.
Start: The village of Bubwith.

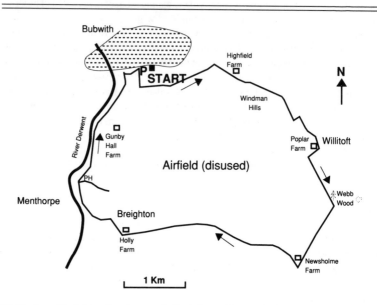

Walk along Breighton Road towards Breighton. Cross a drain and turn left along the footpath by its side to reach the disused railway. Turn left to reach the B1228 close to the Hide Away Inn. Turn right along the B1228 and take the road left to Willitoft at the junction. After passing a sharp left-hand bend, reach a footpath on the right, towards a line of trees. At the corner of these, ignore the path left, and continue forward along the track to Elder Farm.

The path here is shown as passing through the hedge but may still be obstructed by it. Follow any County Council waymarks here if present, otherwise turn right in front of Poplar Farm and then left through the wooded area to reach the track. Take the right-hand gate of two, and walk along the fence side almost southerly. Cross a fence and continue straight ahead towards the trees. Cross some stiles and a plank footbridge. Walk to the road and turn right to reach the B1228 again. Turn right, walking along the grass verge, and round a left-hand bend to reach a track at the next bend.

Follow this and then turn right to follow the field edge. Reach a corner and pass under wires to reach a very narrow track between bushes on the right. Soon a marker shows where to turn right to a footbridge. Cross this and bear left over the field towards the right of a line of small trees and a water tower to reach a track. Continue straight ahead where the track turns right. Pass four trees on the left to reach a hedge. Walk along the left-hand side of this and continue straight ahead to pass Holly Farm and to reach **Breighton**. Turn right along the road and go left at the junction. Take the track at the corner to reach Breighton Ferry Inn by the side of the River Derwent. At the right of the inn, take the embankment top footpath and follow this, passing under the arch of the disused railway bridge, to reach **Bubwith** at the church. Walk through the churchyard and turn right to Breighton Road and the start.

POINTS OF INTEREST:

Breighton – Only small, but with a few interesting buildings. The airfield is now well used by light aircraft.

Bubwith – A large, agricultural orientated, village with the pleasantly situated All Saints' Church.

REFRESHMENTS:

The inns along the route all supply refreshments.

The Hide Away, Bubwith (tel no: 0757 288070).

The White Swan, is on the main road in Bubwith. (tel no: 0757 288209).

Walk 72   BUBWITH – ROUTE 2   9m (14.5km)

Maps: OS Sheets Landranger 105; Pathfinder SE 63/73.
Very flat along riverside, disused railway, and field paths.
Start: The village of Bubwith.

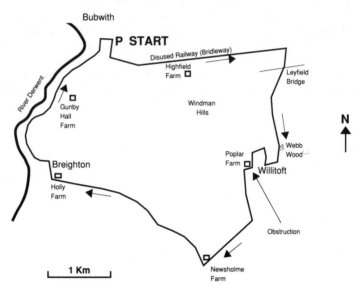

Walk along the Breighton Road towards Breighton. Cross a drain and turn left along
the footpath by its side to reach the disused railway. Turn left. Cross the B1228 close
to the Hide Away Inn. Continue along the track to reach a path from Harlthorpe one
field before a pylon and turn right through a double wooden gate. Cross directly over
the first field, turn right to reach a bridge over the drain, and turn left again to walk
with the hedge on your right to reach a line of trees. Bear left across the next field, or
use the field edge if obstructed, towards the left-hand side of North Covert Plantation.
Pass through a small gate and continue alongside the trees to reach a gate. Bear right
and pass to the left of Willitoft Hall. Go through the gate ahead, turn right along the
hedge side and go over stiles to reach a road.

   Turn right, past Prospect House, and soon take a footpath, left. Turn left along a
track at the field end and, if still obstructed by a hedge ahead towards a track, turn right

in front of Poplar Farm and then left through the wooded area to reach the same track. Take the right-hand gate of two, and walk along the fence side almost southerly. Cross a fence and continue ahead towards trees. Cross stiles and a plank footbridge. Walk to the road and turn right to reach the B1228 again. Turn right, along the grass verge, and round a left bend to reach a track at the next bend. Follow this and then turn right to follow the field edge. Reach a corner and pass under wires to reach a very narrow track between bushes on the right. Soon a marker shows where to turn right to a footbridge. Cross this and bear left over the field towards the right of a line of small trees and a water tower, to reach a track. Continue straight ahead where the track turns right passing four trees on the left to reach a hedge. Walk along the left-hand side and continue straight ahead at a corner to reach a track to the left of the hedge ahead. Pass Holly Farm to reach Breighton (*see* Walk 71). Turn right along the road and left at the junction. Take the track at the corner to reach Breighton Ferry Inn by the side of the River Derwent. At the right of the inn, take the embankment top footpath and follow this, passing under the arch of the disused railway bridge, to reach Bubwith church. Walk through the churchyard and turn right to Breighton Road.

REFRESHMENTS:
Inns along the route all supply refreshments.
The Hide Away (tel no: 0757 288070).
The White Swan, is on the main road in Bubwith. (tel no: 0757 288209).

Walk 73   **HOWDEN**   10m (16km)

Maps: OS Sheets Landranger 105; Pathfinder SE 62/72 & 63/73.

A very flat walk through farmland and along the River Ouse bank..

Start: The car park south-east of Howden Minster.

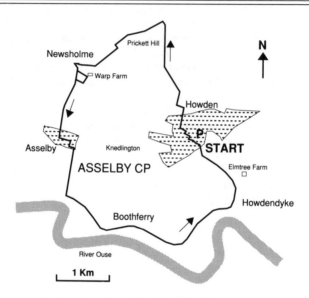

From the car park walk along the path by the side of what was the bishop's palace to reach **Howden Minster** and the small market place. Turn left along Churchside to Bridegate. Turn right and note the memorial ahead before turning left along the A63, Selby, road. After right and left bends you reach a wide track on your right. This passes a barn and narrows. Cross a footbridge and turn left. Pass a drain and then cross a stile on the right. Walk to the far left corner of the field. Cross the stile and turn left. Cross a track and change to the left-hand side of the hedge. Reach a line of trees and a footbridge. Pass between the trees and turn right, over a stile, and go along a narrow woodland path, to emerge into a field.

Walk ahead along the left-hand side of the hedge to reach Brind railway crossing, but do not cross. Instead turn sharp left along the wide track to a low mound, once

154

Prickett Hill. Waymarks should guide you in the middle of this field: continue straight ahead for a short distance, then turn left and quickly right and cross the field aiming for where the left-hand set of wooden electricity posts reaches its edge. Cross into the next field and walk on the left-hand side of the line of trees ahead. A track is reached to Beechtree Farm and Newsholme Village.

Turn right along the road and left along the A63. Cross a stile opposite, and stiles ahead and on your left to reach Warp Farm. Turn right along the farm track. Go over a bridge and turn right along a drain side. Turn left and walk by the side of two trees. Continue ahead to the left of a hedge and, at a corner, bear left across the field to a narrow footpath which goes straight to Asselby. Turn left along the wide track and right to the B1228. Cross to the road opposite by the side of the Black Swan Inn. Turn left at a junction and then right, along a track to reach the embankment of the River Ouse. Turn left.

Pass Asselby Island and keep to the river side of houses at Boothferry. Walk under the Boothferry and M62 bridges and continue past the factory at **Howdendyke** along a track. Turn left over a stile just before a small bridge and houses. Use stiles to cross the access road and follow the left-hand side of the drain between hedges. Turn right in a field and cross a footbridge. Cross the road to the pavement and walk along this going over the M62 to reach Howden. Pass a restored mill house. Cross the A614 and follow the road opposite up to the car park.

POINTS OF INTEREST:

Howden Minster – Partly ruined, is a beautiful medieval church, with a prominent tower. Worth exploring.

Howdendyke – Well inland, has wharves for merchant shipping.

Walk 74   **POCKLINGTON**   11m (17.5km)

Maps: OS Sheets Landranger 106; Pathfinder SE 84/94 & 64/74.

A flat walk including a canal side and a beautiful wood.

Start: The bus station, Pocklington.

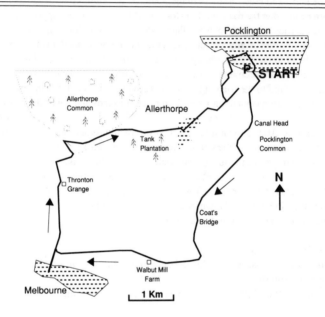

Walk past the old station building, turn right down an alley and left at a road. Near its end, reach a footpath on the right. Take this along the side of a cemetery. Cross the next field bearing to the left of the large buildings and reach a stile in the left-hand corner. Bear left through a gateway and follow the left-hand side of the field. Turn right to reach a stile. Bear right in the next field to reach a stream side. Devonshire Mill is on your right. Follow the stream side to reach a farm at **Canal Head**. Pass through the gates, between buildings, to reach the A1079. Turn right and soon cross to the picnic site.

Follow the towpath of the canal. The path becomes grassy and the canal becomes clearer of weeds. Disused locks and three road bridges are past before Melbourne Ings swing bridge is reached. Across, Melbourne village and the Cross Keys Inn may be reached. We turn right to a footbridge over The Beck. Follow a track which bears left

156

parallel to a fence. Pass through a gate on the right and walk round the field boundary, left, to reach a bridge. Cross the field ahead and continue along the hedge-side track, and ahead at a junction to reach Thornton Grange where beautiful turf is grown. At the farm the path bears slightly right through the farmyard and then slightly left along the right-hand side of a hedge. After passing along the side of three turf fields, turn right, with a hedge on your right, to reach a road.

Turn left and reach the wood at **Allerthorpe Common**. Turn right and follow the bridleway just inside the edge of the wood. Keep to the well-used track. Eventually it emerges into a field and then goes between hedges, past buildings, and turns right to reach a road at the Plough Inn, Allerthorpe. Turn left, pass St Botolph's Church and reach and cross the A1079. Turn right and then left towards Pocklington. Soon turn left to the Gliding Club and walk past the hangars. Before crossing the main runway look carefully to see if gliders are being winched or towed into the air. Avoid winching wires across your path. Aim to the left of a group of trees and follow the locally used route round the right-hand side of the field to reach Barmby Road. Turn right and right again at a junction. Keep right along the main road to reach the car park.

POINTS OF INTEREST:
Canal Head – A pleasant picnic area by the disused canal.
Allerthorpe Common – Mixed woodland with a nature reserve.

REFRESHMENTS:
The Wellington Oak Inn, at Canal Head (tel no: 0759 303854).
The Plough Inn, Allerthorpe (tel no: 0759 302248).
Café on the A1079 (tel no: 0759 302087).
All provide good meals.

Walk 75   **WELTON DALE**   4m (6.5km)

Maps: OS Sheets Landranger 106; Pathfinder SE 82/92.

A picturesque village with a large mill pond, tranquil secluded dale and views across the River Humber.

Start: The Green Dragon, Welton Village.

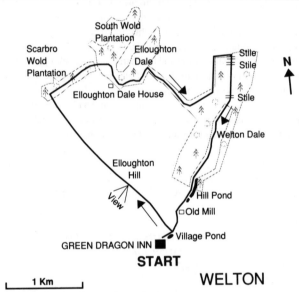

Proceed northwards through the village past the many attractive cottages and a pond to the junction of four roads/lanes. Turn left up the road marked for Elloughton and climb up Elloughton Hill from where there are good views of the River Humber. Descend the road and continue past the left-hand turn for Elloughton. Continue in a straight line passing to the left of the two houses on the right-hand turn of the road. Follow this track up to Scarbo Wold Plantation. Enter the plantation and follow the wooded path up until you enter the larger South Wold Plantation.

Follow the path as it descends steeply to reach a minor road. Cross this and turn left up Elloughton Dale. Follow the minor road for 400 yards before entering Elloughton Dales Woods. Climb the steep bank using the steps and follow the wooded path in a straight line as it continues through the plantation. Curving left, the path descends on to a minor road. Turn left and continue on the opposite side for 400 yards to reach a cemented private road. Turn right and follow the field side path until you reach a stile and waymarks for the Wolds Way. Cross the stile and the cemented road before crossing another stile into the woods. Follow the woodland path into Welton Dale, eventually emerging into a grassy dale. Follow this down until you reach Dale Road. This leads down past the **Mill** and **Cattle Well** back into **Welton** and the **Green Dragon** starting point.

POINTS OF INTEREST:

The Mill and Mill Pond – The mill ceased operating in the 1960s. The water wheel was 36ft in diameter and had 120 buckets attached.

The Cattle Well – One of the numerous wells that gave Welton its name. The residents of Welton still have the right to take water from it.

Welton – A picturesque village with many fine houses and cottages. A guide book of 1841 described Welton as being shielded from chilling winds but open to the southern sky, a remarkably salubrious spot where persons in a delicate state of health find a short stay beneficial.

The Green Dragon – Famous for its connection with Dick Turpin. Turpin moved to this area from where he originally lived in Essex. Adopting the name of John Palmer (Palmer being his wife's maiden name) he began work as a horse dealer, horses which he is said to have stolen in Lincolnshire and driven across the Humber at low tide. He was arrested and interned at the Green Dragon Inn for shooting a game cock in the village street. Despite escaping he was caught and sent eventually to York where he was found out to be Dick Turpin and consequently hanged in 1739.

REFRESHMENTS:

The Green Dragon Inn, Welton (tel no: 0673 666700 or 0673 667493). Lunch served till 2pm.

Maps: OS Sheets Landranger 101; Pathfinder TA 07/17 & 27/37.
Easy walking, excellent for the bird watcher.
Start: The pond, Bempton.

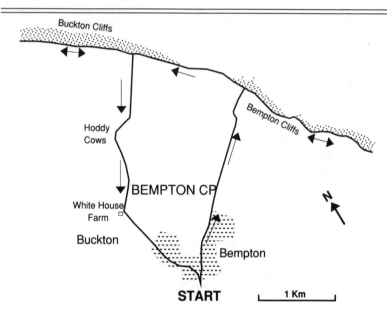

Cars can be parked in Newsham Hill Lane, south of the church and near the pond. From there walk along Church Lane past St Michael's church and go straight across at the cross roads. The road leads directly to the **RSPB Bird Reserve** at Bempton Cliff. It can become a little tedious but, at the right time of the year, this will be quickly forgotten on your first sight of the birds. Turn left along the cliff top, pausing to observe safely in the viewing areas provided.

    After passing through a gate and crossing several stiles, a slightly hilly field is reached. Go across to a stile and signpost. Turn left without crossing, with the fence on your right. Cross a stile and at the end of the next field turn right, through animal pens, to enter Hoddy Cows Lane, a green lane. Follow this as it bears left to reach the B1229 by the side of a pond at Buckton. Here an information board gives an explanation of the unusual name of the lane. Turn left and walk back to Bempton along the pavement.

After passing the petrol station, turn right down Gillas Lane to return to the pond.

POINTS OF INTEREST:

For those who really do not enjoy road walking, cars can be parked at the Reserve. Short walks along the cliff tops in both directions are greatly enjoyed by bird watchers and you may like to add on a little. To the east you can walk up to the northern end of the Danes Dyke earthwork, and to the west a walk up to the triangulation point at the top of the highest cliff on Flamborough Head is worth the effort. Both points give good views across the headland.

RSPB Bird Reserve – At Bempton Cliff. This is possibly the finest reserve on mainland Britain particularly with its gannetry. The 400ft cliffs provide nesting sites for almost 200,000 sea birds. Kittiwakes, razor bills, guillemots and puffins add to the gannets. There is a constant noise – and smell! The birds can be very nearly touched and provide an extremely spectacular flying display below you. Wardens are present from April to August and there is a small information centre usually open during summer weekends.

REFRESHMENTS:

The White Horse Inn, situated at the corner of the lane to the reserve (tel no: 0262 850226).

Walks 77 and 78 HUMBER BRIDGE 5m (8km) or 12m (19km)
Maps: OS Sheets Landranger 107; Pathfinder TA 02/12.
Easy walking with a little climbing.
Start: The Humber Bridge car park at Hessle.

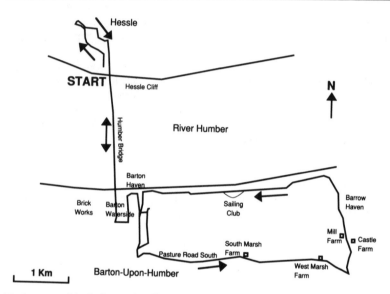

To the west of the **Information Centre** in the car park, follow a track past a **Humber Bridge Park** notice board. Go down a few steps, through a gate and along to a viewpoint sign. Take in the view, then return to descend the nearby steps. Turn right at the bottom. Steps to the left lead down to a pond. Follow the track by its side, and other tracks, signposted to the Humber foreshore, walking westerly to reach an area known as Little Switzerland. Turn right and pass through two tunnels to reach the River Humber. Look out for the partly restored chalk mill. Return through the tunnels and climb the steps ahead. Cross the road and follow the path to the right up to the eastern walkway of the bridge. Hopefully both walkways will be open. As you cross the bridge note the brickworks on the Barton side and the water-filled clay pits.

At the end of the bridge descend to the road, cross and walk under the bridge. Take the footpath on the left and, just before the houses, pass a naturalised clay pit pond, and reach the river bank. Turn right for the at **Barton Clay Pits** Information Centre. For the shortened walk retrace your steps from here.

For the longer walk take the road to the east of the centre and walk along the Haven to reach the station. Turn left along the road past the station. Cross junctions maintaining your easterly direction, and continue forward along the footpath reached, going by the side of a farm and through fields. Go straight ahead at a road and turn left at a junction. At the railway in Barrow Haven, turn left across its bridge. Look carefully first for trains. Immediately turn right along the path to the foreshore. As you return along the river side to Barton, you will be able to see the several different uses to which the claypits have been put, as well as another brickworks. Barton Haven is reached by the side of a disused chemical factory. Follow the track round and take a path left down steps which turns right by a rope works. Note the rails and the long shed. Reach a road that returns you to the station. Turn right and take the first road on the left to return you to the Humber Bridge. Take the eastern walkway. As you cross, note Hessle Haven, start of the Wolds Way, with its shipbuilding cranes. In the far distance you may see one of the massive North Sea ferries. Descend and return to your car.

POINTS OF INTEREST:

Humber Bridge – The 1410m long single span bridge is the longest ever built and takes about half an hour of steady walking to cross. Building began on the site, 5 miles west of Kingston-upon-Hull, on July 27 1972. It was officially opened by the Queen on July 17 1981. Total length of wire used: 71,000km (44,000 miles). The **Information Centre** – In the North Bank car park is open from 9am–4pm weekdays and 9am–6pm Sundays during the summer and a little earlier in the winter. The car park café is open daily in the summer and weekends in the winter. Closing time varies according to weather and amount of custom.

Humber Bridge Park – Has been developed from a disused chalk quarry.

Barton Clay Pits – Have many recreational uses and provide habitats for a wide variety of wildlife. They are the relics of the brickworks. Three works remain active, two of these in Barton. The Information Centre is open during the summer, weekdays 9am–5pm, weekends 10am–6pm. The centre is the start of the Viking Way.

REFRESHMENTS:

There is a café near the mill on the north foreshore and refreshments can be obtained from a stall in the South Bank viewing area car park.

Walk 79   SKIDBY   6m (9.5km)

Maps: OS Sheets Landranger 107; Pathfinder TA 03/13.

An easy walk, with some gentle hills, along field paths and tracks.

Start: The car park at Skidby Mill.

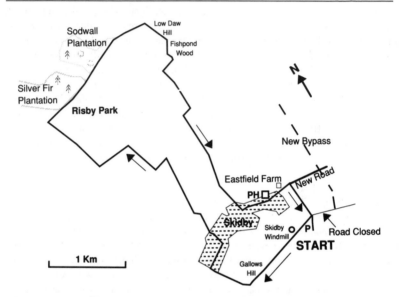

Walk along to the **Windmill** entrance and cross the stile to the footpath heading west. Soon after a small group of trees are reached at Gallows Hill, turn right at the path junction and follow the track downhill to Skidby cemetery. Turn right along the road up to the Little Weighton road junction. Turn left, cross the road, and take the left-hand of the two footpaths to follow a wide track uphill. This narrows into a footpath still following the field boundary. Cross a stile, turn left by the hedge side and right at the field corner. Go down to the minor road ahead.

Turn left along the road. Turn right, through a gate, and walk along the bridleway towards Risby Park Farm. Turn right again after passing through the gate reached just before the farm. The path continues uphill by the side of a plantation. Pheasants are usually seen here. An open area is reached after crossing a stile. Continue straight ahead, keeping the field boundaries on your left, until the Walkington road is reached.

Turn right and walk as far as the bend in the road. Here a footpath crosses a field going up to the left-hand side of Fishpond Wood. Keep to this edge of the wood up to the minor road. Cross the road to the bridleway slightly to the left. Follow this wide track until it eventually passes along a hollow between trees. You may have to walk a little to the left to enter this section. Cross the stile at the end of the trees and continue ahead with the field boundary on your right. Cross the stile and, ahead, arrive at the village hall opposite St Michael's Church.

Turn left along the road. You will pass the Half Moon Inn just before reaching a crossroads. Turn right and continue along the now by-passed Beverley road back to the car park.

POINTS OF INTEREST:

Skidby Windmill – This well restored windmill is open to the public, April to September (10am–4pm Tuesday to Saturday and 1pm–4.30pm Sundays), in Winter (Monday to Friday only). The mill can be seen working on alternative Sundays. Craft shops beside the mill are open daily except Mondays.

A new restaurant and café is soon to be opened next to the mill.

REFRESHMENTS:

The Half Moon Inn – The speciality of the inn is its Yorkshire puddings. Complete with onion gravy, they are a meal in themselves. Well worth a try if you have gained a good appetite walking! (tel no: 0482 843403). Open 11am–11pm daily except Sunday, then 12am–3pm and 7pm–10pm. Children up to 8.30pm. No dogs. Meals 12am–2pm and 7pm–10pm.

Walk 80   **BEVERLEY**   6m (9.5km)

Maps: OS Sheets Landranger 107; Pathfinder TA 03/13.

Almost flat walking, partly through the beautiful and historic town of Beverley.

Start: Park cars in one of the well signposted parks off Walkergate.

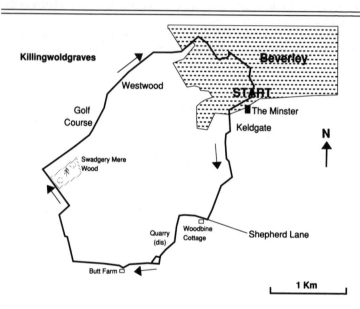

Walk south-east down Walkergate, along Butcher Row, through Wednesday Market and Highgate to **Beverley Minster**. Turn right, left, and right again into Keldgate. Just past the Beehive pub, Kitchen Lane goes off on the left. Continue ahead along the footpath as the lane bends. At the junction with Butt Lane, keep left, walking in a southerly with new housing on your right. **Keldgate Nature Reserve** on the left is followed by the junction with Willow Lane. After two more field boundaries, turn right at the path junction, into the next field and left through a gap in the next hedge and maintain direction until there is a hedge on your right and you reach Shepherd Lane. Turn right to the A164 and cross with care. Building work may cause some problems on this section.

    Turn left along the road and bear right where the old road leaves the new one before a road bridge. Take the track on the right to Butt Farm. At the farm, turn right through a gate and walk by the side of a small drain until you reach a footpath junction with a footbridge on your left. Turn right along the hedge side and reach a bush-lined track. This bends left and quickly right before you reach the Walkington road. Cross the bypass bridge and the road and follow the bridleway by the side of the bypass until a stile is reached on your right. Cross this and walk along the hedge side until this bends to the right. Here pass through the gap on the left and cross the stile on the right to enter **Beverley Westwood**.

Beware of golfers! Walk ahead along the shallow valley keeping a little away from the minor road up to the Beverley-York road junction. Walk along the roadside footpath to traffic lights. Turn right through **North Bar** and, perhaps after pausing for excellent ice-cream, pass **St Mary's Church**. Go straight ahead into the Saturday Market, noting the Market Cross. Where the market place widens on the left, take Dyer Lane back to Walkergate and your car.

POINTS OF INTEREST:

Beverley Minster – A magnificent and well restored Gothic building dating from 1220. There is a treadmill inside.

Keldgate Nature Reserve – A small area maintained by the Yorkshire Naturalist Trust. Springs provide a good habitat for marsh loving plants including irises.

Beverley Westwood – One of five commons here. Very well used for recreation and dotted with grazing animals.

North Bar – One of the original gates. A plaque shows its cost.

St Mary's Church – Small but beautiful, and well worth exploring.

REFRESHMENTS:

There are plenty of cafés and inns to obtain refreshment, mainly close to the market place.

Walk 81   **HORNSEA**   6m (9.5km)

Maps: OS Sheets Landranger 107; Pathfinder TA 04/14 & 24/34.
A flat walk through Hornsea and around the Mere.
Start: The Police Station, Hornsea.

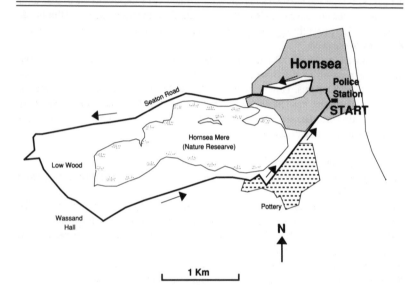

Walk across the road and go north to the entrance of the Memorial Gardens. Continue to the steepled United Reformed Church. Turn right into Cliff Road and cross to the entry to Hall Garth Park. Note the iron gates here. Take the grass track to the left of the kiosk and quickly bear right between trees. St Nicholas Church is on your left, to the east of which is the **Hornsea Museum of Village Life**. The path narrows for a short distance before reaching the road opposite the pretty White Cottage. Turn left towards Market Place and right into Westgate. Walk about a mile along this road, the B1244, using the footpath. There are occasional glimpses of **Hornsea Mere**.

    A footpath signpost and a stile are reached on the right part way round a left bend in the road. Cross the stile and walk uphill, a little to the left of the two wooden power line posts. Just to the right of a farm there is a stile. Over this, the path continues straight across two fields and along the hedge side of a third before joining a track to the side of Buttercup Farm. Continue straight ahead where the track turns left and walk through two more fields with the hedge on your right to reach a road. Turn left to the B1244 and left along the footpath by its side.

The tarmacked and beautifully tree-lined drive to Wassand Hall is soon opposite. Follow this up to a group of buildings and keep straight on here along a gravel track. Wassand Hall is seen behind and on the right. Pass through several gates to reach a gate with a long hedge on either side. Pass through, turn left and then bear a little right towards a stile. A very clear grass path takes you across stiles to the side of the Mere. There are good views of Hornsea across the Mere.

After passing through a gate, continue ahead to reach the Hull road at a gate near the far right-hand side of the field. Cross the road and maintain direction. A wide track is found on your left soon after passing an avenue. Walk uphill past allotments and the disused railway, now a bridleway to Hull. Keep ahead to enter Marlborough Avenue and turn left to the Withernsea road junction. **Hornsea Pottery** is to the right along here. Cross and take the footpath up a little hill, between bushes, to the disused railway embankment. This reaches the nicely converted old station. Walk by its right-hand side to return to the start.

POINTS OF INTEREST:

Hornsea Mere – The largest lake in what is still regarded as Yorkshire. There is fishing, sailing and rowing as well as a very large assortment of water birds. There is also a café. The RSPB visitor centre is open at the weekends. Parking is available and access is well signposted along the Hull road south of Market Place.

Hornsea Museum of Village Life – In the old Burn Farm. Though small, it has won awards. Open daily 10am, Sundays 2pm–5pm. It is in Newbegin not far east of St Nicholas Church.

Hornsea Pottery – This has become a large Leisure Park with a factory shop, displays, shops, a café and restaurant. Open from 10am daily to 5pm or 6pm on Sundays.

REFRESHMENTS:

Available at a wide assortment of places in Market Place and Newbegin, with good fish and chips at Sullivan's Cafe near to the main sea front car park.

Walk 82   **WELTON**   7m (11km)

Maps: OS Sheets Landranger 106; Pathfinder SE 82/92 & 83/93.
A fairly easy walk, partly through woodland. Some of the Wolds Way is used.

Start: The Green Dragon Inn, Welton.

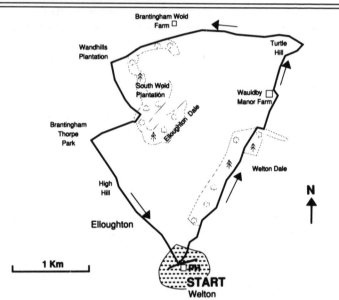

Walk northwards by the side of the small stream to Dale Road and the Wolds Way. We follow the latter for several miles. Note the 'right to get water' notice, the mill (*see* Walk 75), and the mill pond on the right before reaching the gate into the dry **Welton Dale**. Pheasants abound as you walk up the dale alongside a plantation. Pass through a gate between trees and follow the path as it leaves the track to the right. Cross a farm access road and a stile. Turn right for a few yards along a bridleway and then left on a footpath between trees.

Continue in the open field reached, alongside a plantation to Wauldby. At the track junction here, by the side of Wauldby Dam pond, turn left and quickly right along the track in front of cottages. Unfortunately a slurry pond has to be passed! At the next track junction turn left down a bush-lined track. This can get muddy. A road junction is

170

reached. Cross over one road and continue along the road opposite up to a bend. The track ahead leads to the top of Spout Hill and there are good views to the west and towards the Rivers Humber and Ouse.

Cross over the stile on the left and go a short way down the hill. Here we leave the Wolds Way and enter a plantation. Follow the clear path up to a wider track. Turn right. Ignore the path on the left and walk between trees to a gate. The track turns left downhill to reach a second gate. A small Quaker cemetery is passed on the right.

Take the road straight forward up the hill ahead, pausing to see the good views before descending downhill back into Welton (*see* Walk 75). Turn right to **St Helen's Church** and return to the start.

POINTS OF INTEREST:

Welton Dale – The footpath through the dale was the subject of a long, antagonistic, and expensive battle won by the RA, Wauldby. The Manor can be seen at the far side of the pond, as can the now disused church.

St Helen's Church – Very prettily placed. In the north of the churchyard can be found the grave of a lucky man who had eight wives!

REFRESHMENTS:

The Green Dragon Inn, (tel no: 0673 666700 or 667493). The food is quite popular locally. Open weekdays 11am–3pm and 5pm–11pm. Saturdays 11am–11pm. Sundays 12noon–3pm and 7pm–10.30pm. Meals at lunch and evenings. Children welcome.

BRACEY BRIDGE 7m (11km)

Maps: OS Sheets Landranger 101; Pathfinder TA 06/16.
A flat but pleasant walk using field paths, tracks and quiet roads
to link three historic villages.
Start: The Bracey Bridge picnic area on the A166.

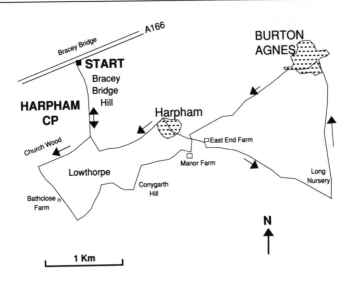

Go south along the track with 'Private Drive' notices. There are footpath signposts!
Bear right along a grass track near to where a pond and an old mill come into view. This
hedgeside track narrows and crosses open field to two stiles. Cross both and walk right,
along the fence, to Church Wood and the **Lowthorpe** road. Turn left along the road and
pass the church. Look carefully at the fascinating cottage just before a telephone box
and stile. Cross the stile and the centre of the field to a footbridge. Bear slightly left to
a gate near the right-hand corner of the next field. Pass through, turn left and quickly
right along the right-hand side of the fence. Cross a footbridge and soon another on your
left. Pause at Lowthorpe Beck then cross a third bridge. Turn left on the Harpham road.

Cross the bridge over Rattling Water and take the path diagonally across the field
to a footbridge. Cross and bear left over the remains of a moat to a stile. Go over to reach

Harpham church. Pass by the side of the Drummer's Well and turn right at the junction by the church side. Turn left at the road and right at the junction. Shortly after leaving the village, pass St John's Well on your right. Take care going through the railway gates and turn left at a junction to reach **Burton Agnes** by the pond. Turn left along the A166 past the Bluebell Inn and take the cross field path aiming just to the left of the far corner. Cross the stile, turn left to a footbridge and walk straight ahead to a post. Here bear half-left diagonally across the field. Walk along the hedge side and then go straight to a stile by the converted chapel at Harpham.

Walk left along the road and right at the junction past St Quentin's Arms Inn. Bear right at the junction to reach a track, left, after passing the last building. Follow this bridleway over Lowthorpe Beck and turn right through a gate reached just before a narrow plantation. At the stiles previously used, retrace your steps back to the start.

POINTS OF INTEREST:

Lowthorpe – The old church is worth a visit. The beck has trout, and kingfishers may be seen.

Harpham – had a Roman villa. The local squire once was St Quentin. His family were said to be haunted by the ghost of a drummer boy drowned in the well. St John of Beverley was born here. There is an annual blessing service at St John's Well.

Burton Agnes – Has a fine Hall and church. The Hall is open from 24 March to 31 October, 11am–5pm daily.

REFRESHMENTS:

The Bluebell Inn, Burton Agnes (tel no: 026 289 379).
The St Quentin's Arms, Harpham (tel no: 026 289 329).

Maps: OS Sheets Landranger 107; Pathfinder TA 05/15.

A very flat walk along river, stream, and canal sides and field paths.

Start: To the east of the railway station, in Driffield at Riverhead.

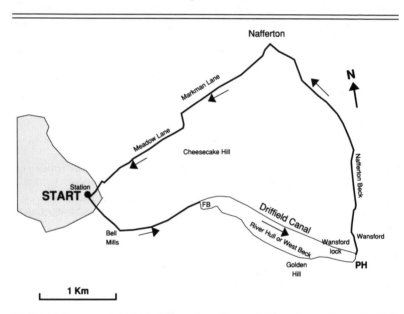

Walk past the converted mill buildings along the canal side and on to the track which passes to the right of Lock View bungalow. The path goes between the disused canal and West Beck, the infant River Hull. Shortly after passing a transformer station and a farm on the road to your left, look along the river side to see if a footbridge is present. A replacement bridge is awaited at the time of writing, and, if it is not yet in position, carry straight on to a bridge over the canal and continue along the road by the canal side to the bridge over the Skerne road at Wansford.

  If the bridge is present, cross the river, turn left and continue along a track by the side of a drain. Go over a stile, past a trout farm and by the side of the wood by Golden Hill Farm. Herons may be seen around. Pass through a gate or over the nearby stile and bear left across a field, at a waymark, to reach the side of the bridge at **Wansford**.

Cross the main road to reach the old mill. Turn left in front of it and go over footbridges to the left-hand side of Nafferton Beck. Follow the beck over stiles to a road. Beware of nettles on this short section. Change to the right-hand side of the beck and, after several stiles, reach a road at **Nafferton**. Cross to the left and take the footpath to the railway. Cross with care. Follow the path which steadily bears left round a field to reach a road in Nafferton. Walk towards the church and pause to see the wildfowl on the Mere. Turn left along Markman Lane (along the south side of the church) and, where this turns right, carry straight on along a track.

Turn left after the first field and quickly right to follow Meadow Lane track to a railway crossing. Again take care. The lane becomes a road. Turn right at the main road, cross and turn left before reaching the level crossing and keep straight on to return to **Driffield** and Riverhead.

POINTS OF INTEREST:

Wansford – A quiet village. Fishing is popular in the river and the canal. Kingfishers may be seen and trout are plentiful.

Nafferton – Has a prominent church and the Mere is surprisingly large. Goldeneye and other waterfowl can be seen along with mallard and often a few swans.

Driffield – A thriving market town. A canal conservation group has been working hard to re-open the canal. Some locks are now usable but, as yet, Riverhead has no boats. A short footpath near King's Mill may be worth exploring.

REFRESHMENTS:

Best obtained in one of the inns in Driffield or Nafferton, or the inn at Wansford. There is a small café in Driffield.

Walk 85   **MARKET WEIGHTON**   7m (11km)

Maps: OS Sheets Landranger 106; Pathfinder SE 84/94.

A slightly hilly walk through pleasant and historic countryside on the edge of the Wolds.

Start: Londesborough Road, Market Weighton. Parking is available close to the toilets.

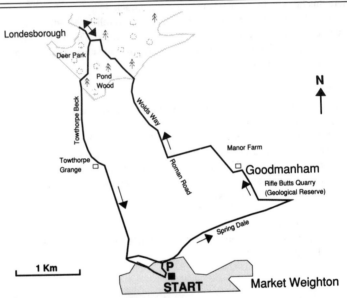

Walk north and soon turn right into Hall Road. Bear left from the footpath at the end and continue along the disused railway embankment, now the **Hudson Way**. Keep to the main track, walk below a bridge and find a footpath on the left which runs parallel to the track along a stream side. Regain the track where steps lead back up. The track crosses a road. Turn left, uphill, along this, now the Wolds Way. The small Rifle Butts Quarry Reserve is soon passed on the right. Turn left at a road junction, and right again at the next. Walk past the church in **Goodmanham** and straight ahead past the Old Hall to reach a track. This, often muddy, track descends, passes over a stream and under a bridge. It then goes steadily uphill, turns right in the corner of a field and reaches the A163 at a picnic site. Cross to the track opposite.

Follow the track to a tarmacked road. Keep straight ahead. Turn left through a gate after reaching a fence, follow the grass track downhill by the edge of Pond Wood and cross a bridge. The lake in **Londesborough Park** is on your left. Keep to the track which bears left uphill. There are views of the Hall. The Wolds Way turns right uphill at a junction. You may like to extend your route here to see Londesborough village and church, otherwise bear left along the track, a public footpath, to reach a gatehouse and a road.

Turn left, and shortly bear right along a track on the right-hand side of trees. The track narrows and Towthorpe Beck is on the left for a short distance. Reach a gate. A high stile is a little hidden on the right. Continue ahead and soon bear left along a grass track and across a bridge over the beck. The track goes to the left of Towthorpe Grange, between a few buildings, and reaches the drive to the A163. Cross to the footpath opposite. The path is almost straight, along the left side of fields, linked by small footbridges. Eventually it bears right and an open field is reached. Cross in line with the telegraph posts to reach the A1079 York road. Turn left and walk through **Market Weighton** back to Londesborough Road.

POINTS OF INTEREST:

Hudson Way – The old railway to Beverley, now a bridleway rich in natural history. Much conservation work has been done.

Goodmanham – King Edwin was converted to Christianity here in 627AD. All Saints' Church is partly Norman.

Londesborough Park – Dates back to Roman times. Railway engineer George Hudson bought the Park from the 6th Duke of Devonshire.

Market Weighton – In the churchyard of All Saints', can be found the grave of the Yorkshire giant, William Bradley, 8ft tall.

REFRESHMENTS:

Can be obtained in a variety of places in Market Weighton.

Walk 86   **BEEFORD**   7m (11km)

Maps: OS Sheets Landranger 107; Pathfinder TA 05/15.
Quiet roads, tracks and field paths through pleasant countryside.
Start: Near the school in North Frodingham Road, Beeford.

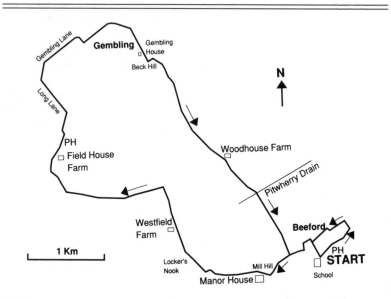

Walk to the A165 crossroads by the Tiger Inn and turn left. Soon turn left down Church Lane, noting the wrought iron shop. The lane becomes a footpath to the church. Walk along the south side of the church to reach Rectory Lane. Turn right and quickly left into the recreation ground. Bear left to a stile and slightly right over the next field. After the next stile, bear a little left to a drain side, and soon cross into a larger field called Gay Chance. Bear left towards a gate close to Manor House Farm. Go through and, soon, through a gate on the right along the drive. Walk half left towards a large, solitary tree and cross two stiles and a footbridge nearby. Follow the side of the drain on the left over a succession of stiles to reach Fosten Lane by Locker's Nook. Turn right along the lane. Go past Westfield Farm, then over an inconspicuous road bridge. Soon go left through a gate and walk straight across the field, though the boundary on the right is unofficially used. The path dips into a small valley. Cross a footbridge and walk along the left side of the hedge to reach a track. Turn right and follow it as it bears left to become the drive of Field House Farm, passing through the very well kept garden, to the road by St Andrew's Church in **Foston on the Wolds**.

Turn right along the lane through the village and left at the junction, into Long Lane. Pass the small school and, at the next junction, turn right towards **Gembling**. The road passes through the hamlet and reaches a junction just past the Manor House. Turn right and go past Gembling House. The lane becomes a grassy track as Northpasture Bridge is crossed and the farm reached. Walk between the barn and the other buildings. Go through a gate on the right and turn left. Cross a stile and follow the hedge side to a stile and footbridge. Cross to the opposite side of the field. Keep ahead along the fence side and cross over into the next field. Walk ahead towards the line of trees and the right-hand side of Woodhouse Farm. Bear a little left, cross the drive and follow the hedge on the left. Reach a metal gate and cross the adjacent stile. Follow the track, right, through a second gate. Where the track turns left, walk ahead over Pitwherry Drain and along the field side to **Beeford**. The path becomes a track. Turn left across a stile used earlier and retrace your steps to Rectory Lane just before the church. Turn right along the lane to the road.

POINTS OF INTEREST:

Beeford – A pleasant village on the busy A165. Close by is Skipsea Castle, a Norman building demolished in the 13th century. There are some large earthworks and good views from the top of the mound. Nearby All Saints' Church, 13th century, is largely built from cobblestones.

Foston on the Wolds – Quiet and well kept. St Andrew's Church dates back many years. The neatly kept churchyard is now almost bare of gravestones.

Gembling – A few isolated houses, a pond, and a wide green add interest to this off the beaten track hamlet.

REFRESHMENTS:

The Tiger Inn, Beeford (tel no: 026 288 733).
The Yorkshire Rose Inn, Beeford (tel no: 026 288 756).
The Plough Inn, Foston (tel no: 026 288 303).
The Board Inn, Skipsea (tel no: 026 288 342).
Warley Cross Café is not too far distant along the A165 South.

Walk 87   **MILLINGTON DALE**   7³/₄m (12.5km)

Maps: OS Sheets Landranger 106; Pathfinder SE 85/95.

A walk over steep hills with rewarding views.

Start: The church, Millington.

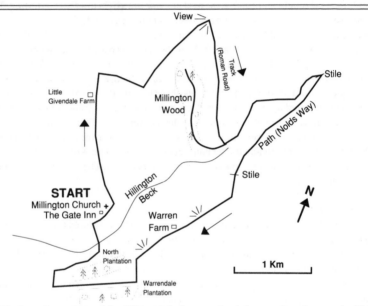

Walk along the main road for 100 yards before turning left on to the minor road which ascends a hill. Follow this road until you reach a junction with another minor road. Cross this and follow the track which leads up to Little Givendale Farm. Continue past the farm for approximately 20 yards before turning right along a field headland (ridge) up the slope of the hill. On reaching a minor road turn left and continue up for about ¹/₂ mile before crossing a road and turning right along a track past Millington Heights. Follow this track as it descends along the course of a Roman Road. On reaching the valley bottom and a minor road you may wish to turn right and follow the road to **Millington Wood** (an ideal spot for a picnic). To continue retrace your steps to where the Roman Road meets the minor road. Continue along the minor road as it enters Millington Dale, looking for a sign for the Wolds Way Long Distance path on your right. Turn on to this and follow the path as it climbs and descends several dales. After crossing Sylran Dale the path follows a field side to where it meets Warren Farm. All along here fine views can be had over the Vale of York and on a clear evening the distant Pennine Chain is silhouetted by the setting sun. To continue, cross the path to Warren Farm and go along the field headland as it turns left and then right across a farmer's field. Cross the field and follow the track as it descends to the right of Warrendale Plantation eventually reaching a minor road. Turn right here and follow the road across Millington Beck and back into **Millington** itself.

POINTS OF INTEREST:

Milington Wood – Formerly owned by the Forestry Commission it now belongs to the County Council. It contains an ancient ash wood and is an important wildlife habitat. A Ranger has recently been appointed and guided walks can be arranged on request (Contact: Director of Leisure Services, Central Library, Albion Street, Hull).

Millington – One of the most attractive of Wold's villages, Millington contains many old cottages and farms which shelter under the steep slope of the Wolds. Its inn, the Gate Inn (where a wide range of real ales are available) is named after the area of land each farmer had in the nearby Millington Pastures. The number of gates awarded to each farmer during the Enclosure Act were proportional to the extent of the land he had before the enclosure in various areas of the parish. In the village street note the 'wheel' set in the pavement. This was the hooping iron used by the local blacksmith to shape the iron wheel rims for carts.

The church has several points of interest not least the squint window through which parish lepers could watch the parson without 'offending' the congregation.

REFRESHMENTS:

The Gate Inn , Millington (tel no: 0759 302045). Serves lunches and has a wide choice of real ales.

Walk 88　　　**WHARRAM PERCY**　　　8m (13km)

Maps: OS Sheets Landranger 100 & 101; Pathfinder SE 86/96.

Along part of the Wolds Way using mainly tracks and field paths and through the pleasant village of Thixendale.

Start: The car park at Wharram Percy Medieval Village.

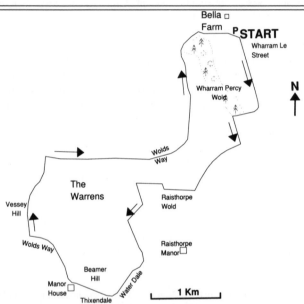

The car park is reached off the B1248 just south of Wharram le Street. It is close to Bella Farm and has a Wolds Way signpost adjacent to it. Follow the Wolds Way south along the very quiet road. After the road bends sharply right continue on the track ahead before it bends left downhill. Pass the southern edge of a plantation. At the next field boundary on your left a footpath runs along the left-hand side of the hedge downhill. Turn right through a gate after the first field on your right and walk along the field edge to reach a track, south-westerly, which passes the southern tip of a narrow plantation. Soon turn right through a small bridlegate and walk westerly to the right of a small depression. Bear right to the end of a hedge. Turn left, westerly, to arrive on a track. At present, this section of footpath is not too clear on the ground.

Walk downhill along the track to the southern side of the second hedge on your right. At the end of this pass through the small gate and bear left, at first above the small valley, and then descending through a gate into it. Continue towards Thixendale parallel to the road crossing stiles before reaching the village. Pass the Cross Keys Inn and a tea garden. Turn right along the road through the village, past the church and the Youth Hostel.

You are now back on the Wolds Way and returning to the start. Take the track uphill on your right. Cross stiles near to an old barn. Go over a fence. Walk left along the field side and go right at the corner and downhill. Halfway down, pass through the gap in the hedge now on your left and continue down to a stile. Climb the hill ahead keeping a fence on your right. Cross another stile and reach a small group of trees and a junction of tracks. Take the track to the right. The valley on your left deepens into Deepdale and, as it bears left, leave the Wolds Way and follow the RA favoured route by contouring along the top of the valley. **Wharram Percy Medieval Village** is clearly seen ahead in the valley. When almost level with the pond, descend to the stile, walk round the northern side of this old fishpond and follow the path to the partly ruined church.

The wide track ahead continues to a bridge, but use the path at its side to cross the disused railway before climbing the hill ahead to reach the car park.

POINTS OF INTEREST:

Wharram Percy Medieval Village – There is plenty of interest here for those interested in archaeology with a great deal of excavation being carried out. Much dates back to Roman times.

REFRESHMENTS:

The Cross Keys Inn, Thixendale (tel no: 0377 88272). Open 11.30am–3.30pm, 6–11pm weekdays, 12–3pm, 7–10.30pm Sunday.
The Red House Tea Room, Wharram le Street (tel no: 094 46455).

Walk 89   **SPURN HEAD**   8m (13km)

Maps: OS Sheets Landranger 113; Pathfinder TA 21/31 & 41/51.

A very flat walk on road, paths and sandy beach.

Start: Spurn Head Nature Reserve.

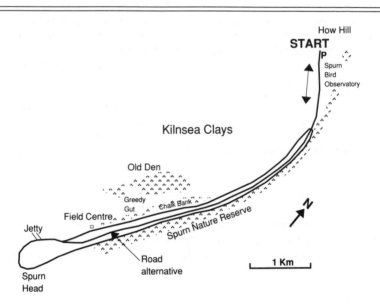

Those who park on the verge before the Head can avoid a 75p parking charge as a Right of Way runs through the car park! Note that no dogs are allowed on the Head, even in cars. Check the weather before deciding which side of the Head to walk first in order to get the best conditions.

Walk along the road past a small information centre for the **Spurn Head Nature Reserve**. The distance between sea and river becomes extremely narrow very quickly and you have three options. Walk along the sea shore, the riverside beach, or the fairly quiet road. It is easy to find paths linking all three. The road passes the base of the lighthouse but it is much more worthwhile using the beaches to round the Head.

Assuming that the beach by the river is used first, descend to this part way along the narrow section and walk along the sandy strip. There is a wide expanse of flat mud exposed at low tide and feeding wildfowl are plentiful. Fishermen also come here to dig for worms. It will seem a surprisingly long time before you pass an old explosives magazine building in the river, and the lighthouse on the Head. A now disused coastguard station is also prominent. Walk under the jetty used by the pilots: several of their small boats are usually moored there. A second jetty goes to the shed housing the Humber lifeboat. This is the busiest, and possibly the most remote lifeboat station, and has the only professional crew in service.

It is not far from here to the tip of the Head. Grimsby lies on the opposite bank, and, on a clear day, the towers of the distant Humber Bridge may just be seen. Forts at Bull Sand and Haile Sand stand, a little distant, in the river. At low tide, many ships may be seen at anchor awaiting the tide. As you round the Head you will again see the lighthouse and the coastguard station. Diversions can carefully be made, avoiding observatories and bird traps, to explore the land near the lighthouse using the network of narrow paths. There are the ruins of several old wartime defences and small sections of rail recall the sail-powered railway that once served the garrison here.

The beach shows signs of the many attempts to save it from erosion. When the narrower and lower section of the Head is reached it is easier to return to the road to reach your car.

POINTS OF INTEREST:

Spurn Head Nature Reserve – Is run by the Yorkshire Wildlife Trust. It is very important for the observation and ringing of migrating birds. The often dense shrubbery and long grass provide a good habitat for varied wildlife. At any time the Head could easily become an island to walk around!

REFRESHMENTS:

The Crown and Anchor Inn, Kilnsea (tel no: 0964 650276).
Any of the three inns at Easington.

Walk 90   BAINTON   8m (13km)

Maps: OS Sheets Landranger 106; Pathfinder SE 85/95.
A slightly hilly walk through pleasant Wolds countryside.
Start: The A163 lay-by on the north side of Bainton.

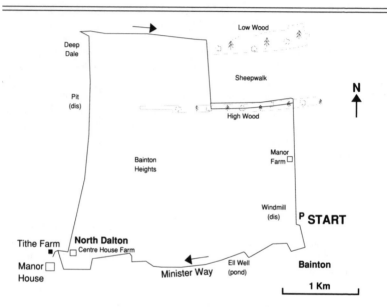

Walk to the church and turn right down the narrow lane opposite to the entrance. Cross the A163 and take the road opposite bearing right and then left past white cottages. Where the road turns sharply right, pass through a gate just to the left and cross the grass field bearing slightly left and just to the right of a line of trees. The field has many earthworks. Reach a kissing gate and turn right in the next field to a gateway. Pass through and immediately turn left to follow the hedge on your left to the side of a small wood. Note Ell Well, a pond, just inside the wood. Reach a gate, cross the farm access track and continue ahead along a wide grassy track. This narrows as it continues in line with telegraph posts and reaches a stile. Cross and turn right to the road. Turn left towards **North Dalton**.

    Pass cottages and an open area on your left and turn left along a footpath just before a line of smaller cottages. Walk ahead over two fields, crossing stiles to reach the corner of a road. Turn right and just before the road starts to descend a little more steeply, turn right along a road. Pass the Post Office and continue ahead to the footpath by the pond. Turn right and cross the B1246. Take the wide track on the left by the side of Centre House Farm and before the telephone box. Follow the track gently uphill through gates and past the sports field and a dew pond. There are good views all round. Eventually the track becomes less obvious as you descend on the right-hand side of the fence to reach woodland.

Pass through the small gate and follow the narrow track through the trees as it bears left downhill to reach a gate on the right. Pass through and turn right along the bridleway in the valley bottom, the ancient Haywold Track. Continue with the fence on your right through two cultivated fields and into a third. Turn right uphill just before reaching the corner of High Wood. At the top corner of the wood a now clearer track continues to reach Low Wood. The bridleway turns left along the northern edge of the wood to reach the B1248. Local people often follow the track which runs parallel through the wood parallel to the road, but it is not a right of way. At the road turn right and continue along the footpath at the side of the A163 to reach **Bainton**.

POINTS OF INTEREST:

North Dalton – The church is perched up on a hill opposite to the pond.
Bainton – The old church of St Andrew's is worth exploring. A socket for an old stone cross is just inside the entrance.

REFRESHMENTS:

The Old School Tea Rooms, North Dalton (tel no: 037 781 618), which has a craft shop.
The Star Inn, North Dalton (tel no: 037 781 688).
Both are near to the pond.

Walk 91   **PAULL**   8m (13km)

Maps: OS Sheets Landranger 107; Pathfinder TA 02/12.

An unusual but often fascinating walk.

Start: The disused lighthouse, in Paull. Parking is available just off the road near the old lighthouse.

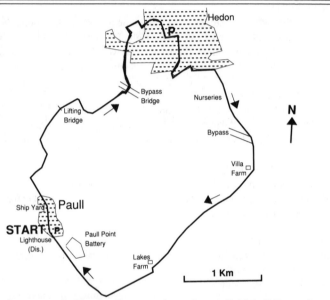

Walk from the car past the Humber Tavern and past the small shipbuilding and repair yard. Take the track off to the left along the Humber embankment. This bends right to follow **Hedon Haven** with the BP complex on the opposite bank. Opposite a cooling tower a small pond, rich in mini-animals, is hidden in an area of rough ground. Cross a road and continue along the bank. Walk underneath the by-pass bridge and turn left across the Haven and a drain. Follow the right-hand bank of the drain north past houses to Hull Road in **Hedon**. Cross straight over and keep to the drain side. Soon cross a road bridge and walk on the opposite bank. Reach a path at a T-junction near a footbridge. Turn left and shortly right, between drains, to reach a footbridge on your right. Cross and walk ahead along the field side to a kissing gate. Turn left down Ivy Lane to reach the Green and the church at Market Hill.

Keep to the left of the church to Soutte Gate near the King's Head Inn. Turn right and walk through the Market Place and ahead along St Augustine's Gate. (Toilets and alternative parking passed on the left.) Turn left at Fletcher Gate, and cross the road to turn right down the bridleway just before the Withernsea road turns right. Cross the bridge over Burstwick Drain and turn left on reaching a road. The end of the Haven is on your right. Quickly turn left again down Haven Basin Road to the Withernsea Road. Turn right and pass a house armed with cannon. Cross and continue along the footpath at the opposite side, keeping ahead at the bypass junction. Shortly after, but before the Thorngumbald boundary sign, cross and follow the rough surfaced Paull Lands Road by the side of a large garden centre and nursery.

Pass Villa Cottage and walk straight along the track to reach Villa Farm. Pass through the gateway and the small gate ahead. Bear very slightly right to a track that is followed to a bridge over Thorngumbald Drain. Turn right without crossing and follow the drain side through open fields to Lakes Farm and Thorngumbald Road. Ducks and other wildlife usually add interest along this section. Cross the bridge and walk along the wide track by the drain to reach a disused lighthouse. Keep by the drain to reach a stile. Turn right along the Humber embankment back to **Paull**. On the way, keep to the higher path where trees and shrubbery hide the remains of **Paull Battery**.

POINTS OF INTEREST:

Hedon Haven – Was once busy with shipping, but now only small pleasure craft are seen.

Hedon – This town was the main Humber port but declined as Hull flourished. St Augustine's Church dates back to the mid 12th century. It is called the King of Holderness, it dominates the area. The Queen of Holderness is Patrington's church.

Paull Battery – Dates back to 1642 when King Charles I laid siege to Hull. Its guns were destroyed but the battery was rebuilt in Napoleonic times, and again in 1862.

Paull – Used to be a fishing village. There are excellent views of the busy Humber, tide permitting, Hull docks with the large North Sea Ferries, and the Humber Bridge. The Trinity House lighthouse, 1836AD, is now a private dwelling.

REFRESHMENTS:

May be obtained at one of the three inns in Paull, or in several inns in Hedon.

Walk 92   **BROUGH–FERRIBY–WELTON**   8³/₄m (14km)

Maps: OS Sheets Landranger 106; Pathfinder SE 82/92.

A scenic walk combining a riverside stroll with woodland paths and minor roads.

Start: At 936264, alongside the British Aerospace works, Brough Haven.

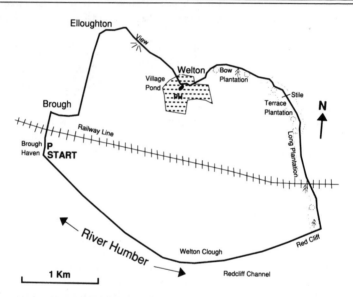

Cross the stile next to the information board, and follow the raised path along the bank of the **River Humber** and next to the airfield. The firm established a base at Brough for testing seaplanes and the old slipway can still be seen. Continue on this path for 3 miles (5km), past the smelting works, along the foreshore until you reach Long Plantation to the west of Ferriby. The Humber Bridge (*see* Walks 77/78) will have been your companion and is best seen from this point. Enter the plantation and join the track which continues northwards as part of the Wolds Way long distance path. Follow its acorn symbol over the railway line and on to the busy A63. The walk continues on the opposite side about 20 yards right of where you exit Long Plantation. Follow the path, through Terrace Plantation as it gently climbs Melton Hill. Where the path meets another continue across until you reach a stile. Cross and follow a path as it curves leftwards and descends to a minor road. Cross the road and enter, through gates, the private Bow Road (access to public allowed). Follow the track up and then either follow the Wolds Way symbol left into Bow Plantation, or continue on the track, both of which meet 600 yards further on. The quarry on the right has reputedly the largest face in the country whilst to the left are fine views of the Humber Estuary. On reaching a quiet country lane turn left and descend into the picturesque village of **Welton** (*see* Walk 75). An ideal stop for refreshments, the Green Dragon Inn (*see* Walk 75). To continue, retrace your steps for 200 yards and turn left on the road marked for Elloughton. Climb the steep road to its rise, from where good views can be had. Descend and follow the road as it turns left, across the A63, into Elloughton. From here follow the road marked for Brough, turning right at the traffic lights to the British Rail Station. Cross the railway line and follow the road back to your starting point at Brough Haven.

POINTS OF INTEREST:

The River Humber – The river drains one fifth of all England's river water and is one of the country's largest estuaries and commercial waterways. It originally separated the two kingdoms of Mercia and Northumbria and now separates Yorkshire from Lincolnshire – though England's newest county Humberside lies on both sides. It is also a natural haven for many varieties of flora and fauna.

REFRESHMENTS:

Numerous pubs in Brough and shops.

The Green Dragon, Welton (tel no: 0673 666700 or 0673 667493). Serves lunches till 2pm.

Maps: OS Sheets Landranger 106; Pathfinder SE 83/93.

A moderately hilly walk, using part of the Wolds Way, along good paths and including some woodland.

Start: On the main street in South Cave.

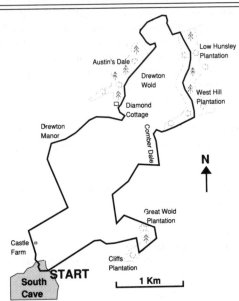

Walk to the crossroads and take the Beverley road. Just before Little Wold Lane a track goes off half-right to a farm. On entering a field, a footpath bears left uphill passing the left-hand side of a group of trees. On reaching a farm track, turn right, follow this between the farm buildings of Mount Airy. There are excellent views from here. Keep to the track, ignoring the Wolds Way on the right. Keep left at junctions and descend to the road. We now follow the Wolds Way.

Turn left along the road and cross soon to the footpath uphill. Turn right along a track continuing uphill through a plantation and going right when you reach a byway. Cross a stile on your left and walk downhill to **Weedley Springs**. The path bears right to a stile. Cross and continue to the right along a disused railway. A track inclines up to the left and a few steps are mounted to join it. Take the clearly signposted track through East Dale plantation, keeping left at a track junction. At the end of the plantation, turn left and follow the field boundary to the road.

Turn left, leaving the Wolds Way, and taking care as this is a busy road. Soon you will reach a gate on your left. Follow the farm track here as it turns left between trees, and then right. Very quickly, turn right again at a junction and walk down the eastern side of **St Austin's Dale**. Note the large rock on the opposite side of the dale, seen just after passing through a gate. When the track reaches a cottage, go through the gate and turn right at the junction. Walk straight along to the main Market Weighton road passing Drewton manor on your right.

Turn left along the road, cross the old railway bridge with care, and use the footpath on the right-hand side of the road. Continue until a cemetery is reached. Cross the stile at the southern end and follow the path along a line of trees. A new golf course has been developed here. The path turns sharply left just before a pond and soon becomes a wider track. All Saints' church and the gatehouse entry to **Cave Castle** are reached. Turn left along the road, passing a fine pond on your left. From the crossroads **South Cave** and the start are easily regained.

POINTS OF INTEREST:

Weedley Springs – An interesting area: the springs seen here did not dry up even in the hot 1989 summer.

St Austin's Dale – The rock is St Austin's stone. St Augustine is reputed to have preached here and early missionaries almost certainly did.

Cave Castle – Dates only from 1791 but is fascinating. It is now a first class hotel and with its own golf course which is also open to the public.

South Cave – Despite its size South Cave was granted the status of 'Town' in 1291 by Edward I. Thus townsfolk were entitled to hold a market every Monday and a one day fair where sheep and horses were bought and sold. By the late 18th century a thriving corn market existed which by 1867 had become obsolete due to the relatively new railways giving easier access to larger markets. The Market Hall, the centre of the corn market, still stands. Built in 1796 the first floor was used as a schoolroom.

REFRESHMENTS:

The Bear Inn, (tel no: 0430 422461).
The Fox and Coney Inn, (tel no: 0430 422275).
The Clock Café and chip shop near to the crossroads.

Walk 94   **WITHERNSEA**   9m (14.5km)

Maps: OS Sheets Landranger 107; Pathfinder TA 22/32 & 23/33.
Gently undulating walking in pleasant countryside and on clifftop.
Start: The promenade in Withernsea.

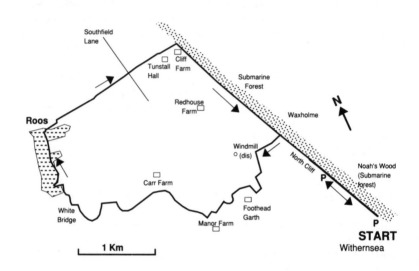

It is usually possible to park in the open space south of the caravan park at the north end of the promenade. If you have not managed this, walk to the promenade, or clifftop, and head north. After passing the caravan park a very small ditch is reached. Turn left along its northern side and continue ahead across a field towards the right-hand side of the hedge surrounding Belle Vue. Follow this round the west side to reach the B1242. Cross slightly to the right and bear left along the shallow drain side. Turn right at the corner to the left of a deeper drain. Quickly turn left along the boundary between open fields. Turn right at the field corner, a little before reaching a telegraph post with a small drain on the left. Turn right along a fence and soon cross a plank footbridge and a stile. Turn right and follow the field boundary round the corner, passing to the north of Foothead Garth and ahead into the next field. Go slightly downhill into the shallow Rimswell Valley and turn left in the corner. Shortly, cross a footbridge and stile on the

194

right and walk ahead through the field to a gate by a farm. Turn right along the track reached and follow this left at the next farm. The track becomes a tarmacked road and reaches Church Road at Rimswell. Turn right through the village, passing St Mary's Church.

At the T-junction ahead, cross over and follow the drive to Carr Farm passing the beautiful shrubbery in front of Dover Lodge and keeping to the left of the farm. After passing a house, continue straight ahead by the side of a tennis court and across the open field towards a small group of trees. Walk round to the south side of the deep drain and turn right, along its bank. Follow this as it bears right and soon left, across a footbridge, and left again at a corner opposite Wood's Plantation. Follow the drain (now called Roos Drain as it turns steadily clockwise and passes the White Bridge. This may be a little easier to cross than the official plank footbridge near the corner ahead. Cross and follow the smaller drain bank towards Roos church. Reach a wider track and soon cross a plank footbridge on the right. Continue slightly uphill towards the church. Turn left to the road in front of the church and enter the churchyard by the kissing gate. Follow the path to the front, and then go left to another kissing gate. Continue along the path and ahead on the road past houses in **Roos**.

Keep ahead at the junction with the main road and the B1242 to pass the Black Horse Inn. Opposite the Roos Arms, turn right along the enclosed footpath to reach open fields. Walk almost straight ahead, with just a few very short left and quickly right turns, along the field edges to reach Southfield Lane. Cross and follow the track up to Tunstall Hall, keeping left at a fork. Bear slightly right to pass Cliff Farm along a road. At the caravan camp, walk very slightly left and then ahead along the camp road to a T-junction. Cross slightly to the right and walk between the stone walls to the shopping area. Note The Mermaid Inn. Take the small gate ahead to the clifftop. Turn right past the boat compound and follow the clifftop or the beach back to **Withernsea**. On the way, note and beware of cliff erosion, and the effect of this as you pass Waxholme.

POINTS OF INTEREST:

Roos – Note the very old cross close to the Church entrance.
Withernsea – A fairly large but quiet seaside resort. The disused lighthouse is now a museum, partly devoted to the RNLI. Open 11am–6pm, weekends April to mid September, and daily during July and August.

REFRESHMENTS:

Available from the inns in Roos, the clifftop Mermaid, and from many places in Withernsea.

Walk 95   **DANES DYKE**   9m (14.5km)

Maps: OS Sheets Landranger 101; Pathfinder TA 26/36 & 27/37.

A moderately difficult walk along clifftops and field paths.

Start: The Danes Dyke car park, reached from the B1255 Bridlington-Flamborough road.

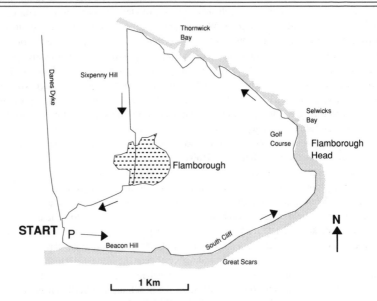

From the car park take the track on the east side which goes down to the shore. After a short distance turn left along a narrower path. Follow this to the clifftop and walk east towards Flamborough Head. Take care and beware of erosion, even though the cliff appears to be very safe. Descend the steps to **South Landing** and go up again by the side of a picnic area. Continue to the lighthouse at **Selwicks Bay**.

The chalk cliffs in the area provide nesting sites for many birds and you may see blow holes and caves. Continue along the clifftop to **North Landing**. The path goes in front of the car park and steps lead down into a gully. Reach a stile in a fence at the top of the other side and turn left. Reach and go behind the bungalows and go along the side of another gully. An easy way across is soon reached. Turn right to **Thornwick Bay**. To the left of the café, take your last climb down and up and walk along the clifftop as it rises steadily. A stile is reached where the fence nears the clifftop. Cross and follow the path with the fence on your left. On reaching a wide farm track, turn left and quickly right, with a hedge on your right, to a stile. Turn right and walk straight through Flamborough village crossing the Bempton road junction. A ruined pele tower is past, a remnant of a fortified manor house. Turn left after passing the church and then right down Water Lane, reached after a pretty cottage. Beyond the gate at the end, a clear path leads back to the exit road from **Danes Dyke**. Turn left and return to the car park.

POINTS OF INTEREST:

South Landing – A few small boats work here. Just uphill along the road is the Heritage Coast Centre and a footpath from the picnic site leads to the Timoneer Inn.

Selwicks Bay – Pronounced 'silex'. A lighthouse and fog siren run by Trinity House, a disused old lighthouse building, and a toposcope giving details of an American War of Independence sea battle involving John Paul Jones add interest to the lovely bay. The café is open during the summer.

North Landing – Has a lifeboat, a large 'smugglers' cave and another seasonal café. A little distance along the road towards Flamborough village is the Viking Hotel.

Thornwick Bay – A pleasant area with yet another seasonal café.

Danes Dyke – Cuts right across the Head, the western end being an Iron Age earthwork. The eastern end has a nature trail and footpaths link to Sewerby Park.

REFRESHMENTS:

Pubs, shops and cafés abound in Flamborough village. Seasonal cafés as suggested above.

Walk 96   **SWINE**   9m (14.5km)

Maps: OS Sheets Landranger 107; Pathfinder TA 03/13.

Easy, almost flat walking along quiet roads, wide tracks and field paths through pleasant countryside.

Start: The picnic site on the A165 road south of Skirlaugh.

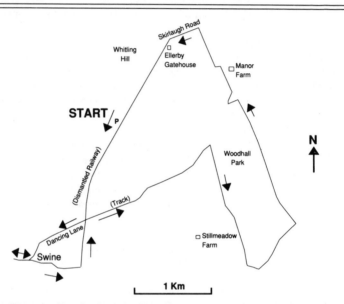

Cross the road and walk along the disused railway line, now a bridleway connecting Hull and Hornsea. Immediately before reaching an isolated house on the right, turn right along the by-way to Dancing Lane which leads into **Swine**. Continue ahead into the village. At the road junction, turn right to see St Mary's Church, passing the Post Office on the way. Return to the junction and turn right, along Coniston Lane. Immediately before the next road junction, turn left, once again on the disused railway line by the old Swine station, and walk back to the isolated house previously passed. Turn right here, along the by-way, Green Lane. Follow this straight ahead to once more reach the A165.

    Cross the road and walk along the much quieter Crab Tree Lane, the Ellerby road. Pass a gas installation and the Woodhall Park gatehouse. Alongside the next group of trees, turn right along a bridleway across a field. Cross the drive to Wood Hall. The wide track soon follows a hedge side and goes almost directly south, eventually becoming a tarmacked lane as it passes by a bungalow and the Still Meadow Equestrian Centre. Soon bear left to reach a corner on the Coniston–Sproatley road. Turn left and walk past the **Woodlands Kennels** complex.

A little way ahead is the **Burton Constable Country Park** but turn left immediately past the kennels, through or by the side of a gate, and walk up Roe Hill through a field with the hedge on your right. Reach Roehill Plantation and walk through to the side of the field to its right before walking ahead along its side. A line of trees by the side of Woodhall Park mark the path side until you reach a wider track which bears right. Turn left off this when you reach Fox Covert plantation. Arrive at an open field and walk straight across to a hedge corner. A telegraph pole and the right-hand group of houses in Old Ellerby help to guide you. Keep ahead to the right of the hedge and soon turn left, through a gap. Follow the hedge and fence side right and left in the corner to reach Old Ellerby opposite the Bluebell Inn.

Turn right along the road past the tiny St James' Church and go straight ahead along Skirlaugh Road at the road junction. Walk along the road past Manor Farm and past several bends to reach the very neatly kept Ellerby Grange Farm and Ellerby Gatehouse. Turn left along the disused railway back to the picnic site, the old Skirlaugh station, bearing right along a narrow path just before reaching it to avoid using the roads.

POINTS OF INTEREST:

Swine – Is a charming little village. The Post Office has a very appropriate sign, and guide booklets can be purchased there about the village and St Mary's Church. The church is kept locked, but a notice at the entry details arrangements for viewing.

Woodlands Kennels – A modern establishment housing greyhounds used for racing at the Hull Kingston Rovers Craven Park Stadium.

Burton Constable Country Park – Privately owned. It is open for most of the summer and has in its collections much of interest, as well as some lovely parkland.

REFRESHMENTS:

The Bluebell Inn, Old Ellerby (tel no: 0964 562364).

Maps: OS Sheets Landranger 106; Pathfinder SE 85/95.
A slightly hilly walk along good paths through, and above, some dry valleys of the Wolds.
Start: The centre of Huggate.

Go north and downhill to reach the track left along the Wolds Way. Follow the track through gates by Glebe Farm to reach and cross the York road. After a short distance, turn left at a junction and follow the path to a road junction. A little way ahead a signpost by a gate leads to the path above Pasture Dale which reaches a small wood. Turn left into this, pass through and turn right by sheep pens and a dew pond. Partly descend to the dale but when the Way turns left, take the opposite direction through part of the wood, cross a stile and descend to the road.

Cross the road to another stile and enter Frendal Dale. Follow the path through the centre of the dale as it bears left through a gate, and then bears left to a small gate into the wooded Tun Dale. The track here reaches a junction. Turn right, uphill, to a road junction. Note the concrete 'Roman' road decorations. Turn right, and then left along the track to Huggate Wold House Farm. Follow the path left and right through the farmyard and continue along the track through gates, eventually turning left and right and descending into Holm Dale to reach the Wolds Way again. A diversion can be made here to **Fridaythorpe** by turning left and following the Way along the central track ahead and then returning.

Otherwise turn right, down Holm Dale. Pass through the gate at the junction with Horse Dale and turn right. Cattle can make it muddy for a few yards here, but the mud can usually be avoided with care. Bear left uphill to reach a small gate and follow the field side footpath to the access track to Northfield Farm. Turn right downhill along this very pleasingly kept track. There are good views of **Huggate** ahead and you soon retrace your earlier steps back into the village.

POINTS OF INTEREST:

Fridaythorpe – Is spoilt a little by the busy road through it, but has a nicely kept pond and a plaque marking the halfway point of the Wolds Way.

Huggate – A pleasant village sheltered in a hollow high on the Wolds. The church spire is often all that can be seen of it.

REFRESHMENTS:

Can be obtained at the Inn, restaurant, or petrol station café in Fridaythorpe.

The Wolds Inn, Huggate (tel no: 0377 88217), popular with walkers. The latter has more of the 'Roman' concrete designs that are dotted round the area!

Walk 98   NORTH NEWBALD   10m (16km)

Maps: OS Sheets Landranger 106; Pathfinder SE 83/93 & 84/94.
A slightly hilly walk on and below the edge of the Wolds, often on pleasant tracks.
Start: North Newbald.

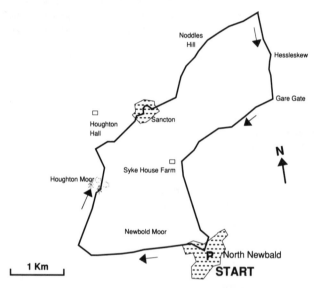

Walk along the north side of St Nicholas Church passing over a stream in Galegate. Bear left into Westgate and cross the A1034 Market Weighton road. Walk along Cliffe Road which becomes an unsurfaced bridleway to Cliffe. **Houghton Woods** ahead are eventually entered. Pass the keeper's cottage. A track crosses in a more open area: turn right at the junction and continue through the woods ignoring all side tracks. Reach a gate and stile on the northern edge. Cross and continue straight ahead, going over two more stiles and through a gateway to reach a road. The grounds of Houghton Hall are opposite and the lake may be glimpsed. Turn right and walk along the quiet road to **Sancton**. Bear left at a junction within the village. Turn right and again reach the A1034. Cross and turn left. Just before the church, a track on the right bears right. Cross a sheep barrier and follow the track as it turns left along the bottom of a shallow dale and climbs gently to a gate. The track beyond goes through a more open field to reach a stile on the left. Cross and maintain direction with a fence on your right to a gate. A farm track goes uphill, but, after only a few yards, bear left across the cultivated field aiming straight for a clear gap in the hedge opposite. The path should be clear through the crop.

Turn right along the road, the Wolds Way, and pass Hessleskew Farm. The road turns right and the Wolds Way leaves it, going straight ahead along a grass track. Reach a hedge at the end of the field on the right and turn right, leaving the Way. Walk with the hedge on your right along a track which bends round the edge of a copse and reaches a gate and stile. Cross and enter the top of a small dale. Walk down along the centre to a stile and enter another cultivated field. Keep the hedge on your left. A rough area is the beginning of a grass track to Syke House Farm. Go through a gateway and turn left just before the farm, going uphill along the good field side paths. Soon there are good views to the west. As some woodland is neared, the path becomes a track with **North Newbald** just below. Cross the road and, slightly to the left, continue downhill between houses to Eastgate. Cross and walk beside the little stream to the Green. Bear left past the inn to the church and start point.

POINTS OF INTEREST:
Houghton Woods – Pleasantly mixed trees. The rhododendrons are a weed here and have been nicely controlled.
Sancton – The old church has an unusual octagonal tower.
North Newbald – A pretty village, a little spoilt by new housing. The old church is worth visiting but may, alas, be locked.

REFRESHMENTS:
The Star Inn, Sancton (tel no: 0430 827269). Snacks.
The Tiger Inn, North Newbald (tel no: 0430 827252). Good meals across lunch time and after 7pm.

LOCKINGTON 11m (17.5km)

Maps: OS Sheets Landranger 106; Pathfinder SE 84/94, 85/95 & TA 04/14.

Gentle walking through pleasant countryside using field paths and very quiet roads connecting peaceful villages.

Start: The lay-by in Scorborough.

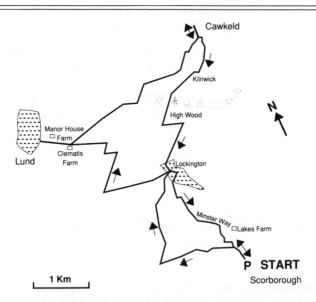

There is alternative parking in Lockington and in Lund. Cross the stile by the entry to Lakes Farm at the southern end of the lay-by. Bear right to cross a farm track and stile and continue ahead to the right of a hedge. Bear right to a concrete track. Turn left and quickly bear slightly right along a bridleway across fields. Reach a hedge and continue along a grass track past the side of a copse. Go through a gate on to a wide track. Turn right and follow this to Thorpe. Turn right into **Lockington**, pass the lane to the church, and turn left down Dead Lane (No Through Road). Pass a field on the left and turn left through a gate into it. Bear half-left and go through the right-hand gate. Follow the hedge side to a stile and use the fieldside path to a road. Turn right, pass a junction, and turn left over a stile after crossing a drain. Follow the field boundary as it turns right to reach a road. Turn left towards **Lund**. Cross the stile just before Clematis Farm after diverting ahead to see Lund.

Walk diagonally over the field to a stile. Maintain direction towards the left-hand corner of a wood. Continue past the corner towards the next corner. Turn right here to reach a road. Turn left and pass Lund Moor Farm and a copse. Immediately turn right and walk with the hedge on the left. Go over a stile and stay with the hedge as it bears left to a road. Cross and follow the drive past Kilnwick House Farm. Continue ahead at a bend, to reach a stile and footbridge. Turn right to go over another footbridge and turn left round the field side to reach a gap to enter the wood. The path, possibly a little overgrown, soon bears right to a wire fence and a stile. Cross the field to another stile. Turn left into more woodland to see the lake at Cawkeld. Return and bear slightly left across the field to a stile. Follow the clear path straight ahead to Kilnwick. Walk past the church and turn right at the junction. Turn left at a gate and cross the field diagonally. Turn left on the track through woodland, then continue with a hedge on the left to a road. Turn left, and right at a junction to Lockington.

Turn left along Front Street, and right along the South Dalton road. Turn left down Church Lane and use the path bearing left round the church to reach a footbridge. Cross and then cross a stile on the right. Walk along the beckside to a stile and footbridge. Ahead is another stile. Go over and bear slightly left to cross two larger bridges. Cross a stile and bear right over the field to another stile. Turn right, and then left along the hedge side, and soon left across the field from the end of the hedge. Turn right and soon retrace your steps back to the start.

POINTS OF INTEREST:

Lund – has won several awards for the best kept village and the national Britain in Bloom competition. Hopefully the Wellington Inn will be re-opened.

Lockington – Also a well kept village. The ancient St Mary's Church is worth seeing.

REFRESHMENTS:
If the inn is still closed, refreshments may not be available.

Walk 100   SOUTH CAVE AND BRANTINGHAM   12m (19km)

Maps: OS Sheets Landranger 106; Pathfinder SE 83/93 & 82/92.
A walk over undulating ground with panoramic views and secluded woodland dales.
Start: At 923313, the crossroads in South Cave.

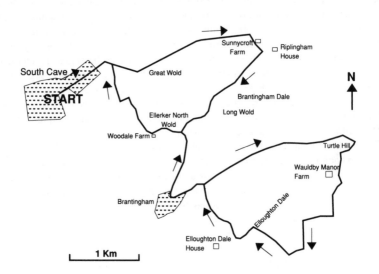

From the crossroads head eastwards up Beverley Road, on the right-hand side, for approximately $^3/_4$ mile. Immediately alongside the last house on your right is a track signed for the Wolds Way. Follow this track up to, and through, Great Wold Plantation. Follow the track to the left along the side of a small plantation continuing along a hedged track to reach a stile. Cross this and follow the fence, left, to the triangulation point. From here to the south you can see the Humber Estuary and the Lincolnshire Wolds. Descend slightly to a minor road at Riplingham, where earthworks can be seen in the farm fields on the opposite side of the road. Turn right and continue down the road for 300 yards before turning right again on to the road marked for Brantingham. Follow this road through Brantingham Dale and into the village of **Brantingham**. You may wish to stop here for refreshments.

To continue, take the road to the right of the road you used to reach Brantingham. Follow this unspoilt green lane known as Spout Hill, again part of the Wolds Way, for nearly $1^1/_2$ miles until you reach a minor road. Cross this and follow the waymarked track through Bottom Plantation. Continue on as it turns right along a headland track up to **Waudby Manor Farm**. Turn left by the farm and then right along the side of the pond. Continue along this field headland (ridge) until you enter a small plantation. Follow the signs to the right and on reaching a stile, do not cross on to the cemented road, but follow the path with the road and hedge on your left to reach a minor road. Turn left here and cross the road. Follow the road down until you reach a woodland path on your right. Enter the plantation and continue on the track for $^3/_4$ mile until you reach some steep steps which will lead you into Elloughton Dale. On meeting the minor road turn left and descend about 400 yards before turning right into the Southwold Plantation. Take a long woodland track, keeping more or less in a straight line, following the left-hand limit of the woods. After approximately $^1/_2$ mile you will emerge on to Spout Hill Lane. Turn left and retrace your earlier steps, re-entering Brantingham Dale, for about $^3/_4$ mile. Keep to your left and you will see the 'Wolds Way' symbol marking the track you should take. Ascend the steep hill and then descend to Woodale Farm. Turn right through the farm and climb along the side of Woodale Plantation and then into it as it turns left towards Mount Airy Farm. Excellent views are obtained here of the Humber and Lincolnshire to the south, and the Vale of York to the west. Follow the farm track and descend to the road you initially started on, turn left, at the main road, to re-enter South Cave (*see* Walk 93) and rejoin the start.

POINTS OF INTEREST:
Brantingham – An early Saxon settlement, though evidence was found of Roman occupation. In 1941, during quarrying, walls, mosaics and tesselated pavements of a Roman villa were found. One of the two mosaics can still be seen in a Hull museum.
Waudby Manor Farm – 100 years ago it had a population of 86 and a small church.

REFRESHMENTS:
Pubs and Shops at South Cave. Lunches till 2.30pm (from 11am).
Pub at Brantingham.